TUNES OF GLORY

What music is good enough for God?

Ian Mackenzie

THE HANDSEL PRESS

Published by
THE HANDSEL PRESS
The Stables, Carberry, EH21 8PY
Scotland

ISBN 1 871828 16 3

Typeset in 11pt. Garamond
Printed by Bell and Bain Ltd, Glasgow

CONTENTS

The Baird Lectures for 1990

For my father, John Kennedy Mackenzie,
who in Cranshaws, Stornoway, Fraserburgh, and Prague,
made the pulpit sing

ACKNOWLEDGEMENTS

I reveal in the text my fundamental debt to those who magicked words and music into my life. As regards the Baird Lectures which became this book I have five acknowledgements to make. Barrie Allcott and Ray Bruce of CTVC fitted filming in Scotland, Prague, and Jerusalem round the dates of the lectures, and put up with my working on them on location; Donald Erskine, Chairman of the Baird Trust, and Angus Sutherland, its Secretary, cheerfully accepted the logistic risks such filming posed, and made the lecture evenings pleasant occasions; Jock Stein of the Handsel Press sympathetically midwifed editorial changes for publication; my colleague, Elizabeth Robin, organised the practicalities of both filming and lecturing before turning her attention to processing and revising the material into book form; and my wife Elizabeth, with my children Stephen and Alice, made the project possible by advising me to retire early from the broadcasting hamster wheel in order to do some proper work.

The hymn by John Bell and Graham Maule on page 160 is printed by kind permission of the Iona Community.

FOREWORD
by the Rt Revd D.E.Jenkins, Bishop of Durham

This book is a lively report of, and reflection on, what must have been a Performance about performing to the Glory of God and the edification, liberation and delight of our hearts, minds, souls and bodies. I do not imagine that this written form of the Baird Lectures for 1990 on Church Music can fully represent the performing of the lectures with the accompanying and additional illustrations on the piano in the Hutcheson Hall, Glasgow and at the organ in Renfield St Stephen's Church when Ian Mackenzie originally gave them. I imagine that the impact was immediate, exciting, provocative, amusing and deeply devotional.

Clearly, it is worth the attempt to convey the content of the lectures and for the written word to do its best to deliver the mood, tone and vibrations of the message - for these are as much the content of the message as the immediate sense of what is written. At least this is what I pick up from the script. It is, it seems to me, wholly in the spirit and purpose of these wide ranging reflections and anecdotes on the interaction between art, music, faith, doctrine and life that the author/performer should have been constrained to add a Prologue and six Epilogues which are addressed as practically as possible to the issues of music in Church, both in its performance and, especially, in its congregational aspect.

There is the greatest possible need to restore the confidence of ordinary people, and of those whom I might tentatively call averagely competent amateur musicians, in our combined capacity to enjoy music in worship, to perform it reasonably well and feel free about it - so free that we do our best to be as disciplined and as competent as we can, while not being put off by the over-pursuit of excellence. One of the bad effects of the media age is to present us with amazingly polished productions and performances which we watch - and often rightly enjoy - but we only watch. Often, we feel de-skilled and discouraged about our own performing and participation. The discouragement is compounded in church circles by the feeling that the only answer to our discouragement is to introduce a specially exciting but peculiar style of music - which soon settles down to a rather narrow range and a very particular style and in so doing tends to become an addiction for those who catch it and an offence to those who cannot stand it.

These lectures range widely and perceptively over the whole range of music and are unashamedly traditional as well as teasingly innovative, or one might say, ready for bad taste as well as good. They should therefore encourage many a minister and congregation where music is flagging to relax and make new and enjoyable attempts at combined and congregational efforts to restore the resonances of music, both sung together and sometimes listened to in our worship.

I believe that the lectures convey such a conviction, and so embody an exemplification of the possibilities of music for restoring depth of emotion, all combined with disciplined participation and the sheer sense of praise and wonder, that they should encourage many to take practical steps to rescue well-intentioned worship services from the near boredom and banality which too often hover around them.

The mysteries of God, the possibilities of persevering love, and the promises of simply living together to share whatever has to be shared, have depths in them which go far deeper than words - no matter how central and essential to our Christian Faith is the Word made flesh and the words of Scripture, tradition and preaching which we have to struggle to communicate, understand and obey. Depth, infinity, wonder and joy must break into our worship and permeate our lives. The praise of God catches us up into possibilities, promises and practices which are at once crucifying and glorious. Music can reflect this - without music the amazing, the wonderful and the dimension totally beyond words is all too often missing. Doubtless, to restore such depth we need not only to renew our music but also to re-develop the proper use of silence and stillness. Ian hints about this too as he reflects, argues, and tells his stories.

So I am grateful for this book, and even more grateful for the performer behind it and the indications of possible performances which it offers to all of us. When preaching at institutions of clergy in my own diocese I tend to speak to congregations of the shared glory, wonder and excitement of Christian Faith and Discipleship. Sometimes I venture to advise the congregation and parish: "And if your new priest and minister starts boring you and fails to give you Heaven, then give him hell (although only in a Christian way, of course!)." I believe this book gives us both inspiration and practical direction about how ministers and congregations can combine, more efficiently and more enjoyably, to share in and witness to, the heavenly possibilities and promises of really down-to-earth praise and celebration of God.

PROLOGUE

In 1989, the Baird Trustees invited me to deliver the Baird Lectures of 1990 on the subject of church music.

These lectures are given every five years, by notable ministers of the Church of Scotland. Although I am a minister of the Kirk, I have not counted myself a notable one, least of all in comparison with giants of communication like the late Professor William Barclay, who gave famous Baird Lectures in the '60s.

However, it was difficult not to be intrigued by the terms of this invitation. They were that in recognition of Glasgow's Year of Culture this lecture series should have a theme relating to the arts, resolved in favour of church music; and that they should be delivered in Glasgow. In view of my career in religious broadcasting, it was thought by the Trust and myself that I would make use of audio-visual aids. Further consideration led to a different conclusion. The Hutcheson Hall, where five of the six lectures were given, is an elegant protected building in the Merchant City, with a fine resident piano, and it seemed more in keeping with that environment that if I had anything to say, I should say it, and if there was music to be heard, I should play it. The sixth lecture was given in Renfield St. Stephen's Church, where I was able to use the pipe organ.

The lectures which form the body of this book are about music in its widest sweep and as such are intended for the general reader.

When they were delivered, an hour's speech at the lectern was followed by half an hour at the piano, of playing, talking, even on occasion a burst of not very charismatic song. The audience seemed to feel that these musical demonstrations were helpful in unpacking the preceding rhetoric. Later, with the help of a resourceful *ad hoc* choir I was able to develop these demonstrations on four Radio Scotland programmes in July 1991.

In adapting the material for publication there was no obvious way of transplanting musical exposition into a verbal text, yet it seemed desirable to adopt some alternative device for earthing anecdotes and showing that my broad conclusions might relate to the everyday world of church music. This prologue is that device. In what follows I venture to encapsulate some practical proposals which are developed at more logical length in the final chapters. This summary can be skipped by readers unscathed by responsibility for the musical *minutiae* of worship. People interested merely in music, God, and life can tune in at Chapter One.

I am indebted to the Baird Trust for their trust and support. The fact that I think the subject is important will, I trust, leak out in these pages. To do justice to it is another matter. What I have sought is at least to offer some reassurance to those who provide or participate in church music in any form. The devotional and musical treasures of the past are still there to be enjoyed, and that is what, above all, we should be doing: enjoying them.

PRACTICAL SUMMARY

What I tried to do in my safaris around the piano at the end of each lecture was to connect general insights about music with specific points about church music, and in particular, about hymns. For example, one conductor's interpretation of Brahms' Third Symphony related to one organist's way of dealing with an Easter hymn. It had been referred to in the lecture, but the penny dropped, I guess, when I was able to draw the comparison at the piano. Similarly, with 'Waltzing Matilda'. That old tune, mutated in the film 'On The Beach' from Antipodean cheeriness to Elgarian *nobilimente*, came into focus when I was able to show how equivalent chord structures in certain Victorian hymns could benefit from equally robust treatment. I further suggested that the show-bizzy, almost operatic nature of such hymns could justify plundering the now obsolete Revised Church Hymnary for 19th Century tunes rejected by the Editors of CH3.

Are such ideas a little recondite for application at the parish coal-face? Quite the reverse.

In my time with the BBC, one question was put to me repeatedly by organists and clergy. Haunted by the judgement that they were failing to provide adequate music in worship, they would ask the devastatingly simple question: how can we improve the singing? This *cri de coeur* impresses in its heartfelt directness more than the more highfalutin' form one has encountered: how, in this day and age, are we to save the Church's song?

However the question is put, it is a simple challenge. Is there a simple answer? Yes, there is. The singing can be improved by means which are spectacularly simple. So simple, in fact, that when I unpacked them in the free-for-all session which concluded the lecture series, there ensued a mildly rowdy debate (good humoured, I hasten to add) between those who thought I was up a creek of startling naivety without a paddle, and those who felt I was the first person to offer them an inexpensive but useable outboard motor to tackle the choppy waters they found themselves in Sunday by Sunday. If I disclose that members of the first group tended to come from churches with well organised choirs, and those of the second category from parishes in less good musical order, that may only serve to underline the relevance of the proposals I now make. Most of these ideas, I promise, are entirely practical. And none of them need cost a penny.

TEN GOLDEN RULES

1 Lower the pitch of most items of congregational praise. And really lower it. If half the choir doesn't raise an eyebrow and a prominent chorister doesn't threaten to resign, you may have not lowered it enough. It'll work? Yes.

(a) Most of the men in the congregation will love it.
(b) Some of them may even start singing.
(c) Some hitherto quiescent women in the pews may join in.
(d) Hey presto - in a month, the congregational singing will be twice as good.
(e) When it is seen to work, the choir will come round.

All at no financial cost whatsoever.

2 Vary speeds of hymns. Vary them dramatically. Take some much slower, others much faster. Trial and error will tell which. At a stroke, this will waken everyone up and give new life to old words and tunes. Nothing is so deadening as a regular brisk *cha cha cha*, or a uniform weary slog.

3 Try at least some hymns, psalms, and songs entirely in unison. Unison in the last verse only is often effective as a climactic opportunity for the organist to splice the mainbrace and vary the harmonies, but why should the poor old congregation not be allowed to let go until the end? Why shouldn't it have the 'lift' of the choirmen and contraltos singing out the tune before the final verse - by which time it is often too late to flog the dead hymnological horse?

4 Vary the loudness of accompaniments. Vary it dramatically. Many organists, sometimes from the spiritually worthy motive of not unduly intruding, keep to a safe middle range of noise level. This becomes as deadeningly predictable as unvarying speeds. Try some verses (even some entire hymns) very quiet indeed. Not dully quiet. Dramatically, excitingly, atmospherically quiet. Some unaccompanied. But take others at full throttle, storming heaven, or hell, or wherever the hymn is at.

I'm reluctant to add this, in case it re-introduces a note of dull caution, but of course one does this intelligently, on the basis of what the words and the tune suggest; and in the context of the whole drift of the worship on the day. Thoughtful consideration of deep mysteries requires radically different treatment from the lively declamation of robust challenges, or a burst of joy.

5 Vary forces and resources. Don't rely on the organ (if you have one). Try out piano, Yamaha, trumpet, tambourine, bagpipes, guitars - whatever is around. Few towns, villages, or city communities lack somebody who blows, scrapes, scratches, or hits things which make sounds. Clergy, organists, choirmasters, leaders of worship, should feel free to use them experimentally. That sounds exploitative: should feel free to enter into lively dialogue with them as to how they might contribute support, atmosphere, excitement.

6 That extends to the choir. The choir needn't be stuck in its conventional role of wrapping hymns up in four-part cellophane. Its jobs include:

(a) Leading congregational singing. That's number one priority. Try placing the choir in different areas of the church building. And vary the menu. Give them opportunities to sing in unison; in groups; in procession; in solos and duets. Or sometimes, just disperse them in the pews.

(b) An occasional spectacular anthem, rehearsed over four weeks till it can be performed with blistering ferocity or melting smoothness, is a hundred times more valuable than one galloped through on thin ice every Sunday. An anthem should be for the congregation a treat, not something to be tholed. Why not periodic services of praise (on top of Christmas and Easter) where the choir (and other musical groups) unashamedly show off what they can do? Nothing wrong with that. It may be showing off God too.

(c) Demonstrating new hymns. This is often done nowadays, and if it is introduced properly, explained fully, handled with a light, yet business-like touch, and followed through by incorporation in the worship, it can pay big dividends all round.

7 Do not be embarrassed to be out of step with what seems to be the fashion. Don't worry about good taste; some may think you old-fashioned, others may think you not old-fashioned enough. Variety is best here, too. There are many acceptable styles. But whatever style you choose, feel free to let it rip. Be confident. I keep saying: be dramatic. What I mean is: take emotional risks. A wrong note doesn't matter. A wrong mood does. A chilly, dull, safe, middle of the road caution is, in terms of worship, always a wrong mood - so, sometimes, is a relentlessly cheery one. What is each service trying to achieve? What is the underlying script?

8 Do not be afraid of the old chestnuts. In particular, why not heave the great Victorian hymns out of the cobwebbed cupboard? Let them rip, too. Raid the old Revised Church Hymnary and any other book old or new that comes to hand. Flowers bloom in odd corners.

9 Organists and clergy: talk to each other. Even better: listen to each other. Best of all, plan with each other. Miraculously, the co-operative contagion might spread, and you would find that you could enlist other groups, church organisations, kirk sessions, the congregation itself, in thinking through ideas. None of this costs money.

10 Feel free. Experiment. Try things. Step off the cliff. Enjoy it!

These suggestions apply to traditional and new music equally. But the point I feel needs making is that while contemporary hymns, songs, and arrangements are seen as inherently experimental, a no less fresh approach is required to animate the 'old' music. It may be objected that all this seems absurdly simple. It is, it is. Yet I wager only one in ten leaders of church worship - in pulpit, or organ stool, or conducting a choir - would have the nerve to implement it. That figure will surely improve as the new lively Music Committee of the General Assembly Panel on Worship expands its missionary work; but that sometimes involves a surrender to new material which not all congregations are ready or suited for. What I am suggesting is that at no financial cost or change of musical tradition, singing in worship can be revolutionised virtually overnight. So why may it not be? Because of a lack of underlying confidence in the expression of emotion. As I say later on, we Scots carry our feelings deep, and often deeply locked up. We do not trust ourselves to be vulnerable. And there is perhaps a more basic lack: a loss of belief in the immensity of what we are doing in worship. It is to that underlying loss of nerve, as I perceive it, that these lectures were in the first place directed. Yes, there are practical implications. But the fundamental question is one of belief. Is God really in music? If so, how does that affect, not only the nitty-gritty practicalities of public rituals, but the depths of our living?

Chapter One

GO FOR GOLD

I had a dream the other night which unstuck my brain. I wrote it down when I woke, so I can report with confidence that what I am about to recount is what I dreamt; though whether that is of any interest is, of course, another matter, one's own riveting dream being potentially someone else's jaw-cracking yawn.

I was walking along Edinburgh's Princes Street. With me was an urbane ex-colleague, Head of Programmes for my first few years in the BBC. A good boss, calmly inclined to say yes to an interesting idea.

"An awful lot of waffle on the air these days", said Pat.

"Wasn't there always?" I asked. Then I added, "Some people used to say I waffled."

"Er, yes, I recall that", he acknowledged.

"But I didn't!" I felt obliged to remind him.

"Not always", he parried.

I knew he was teasing. Well I thought he was. In case of doubt, I spelt it out. "There are three ways of communicating. First, minimally: economical language. No overt style. The 'style' is in the structure, the interior clarity, diamond precision, unadorned logic."

"There you are", Pat said, "three unnecessary adjectives already." I ignored this.

"Then there is language which is pushing the boat out, extending boundaries, stretching words and images, trying to mean something new or make an old meaning accessible in a new way. If we stop that stretching process, we die. On the other hand, of course, by not pushing the boat out we may avoid mistakes, or what strike purists as mistakes?"

"Are you saying", asked Pat, "that pure language is a mistake?" I chose to ignore this also.

"And thirdly, there is waffle. I hate that because it fouls the nest for those of us who are throwing words or music around a bit, for more positive reasons than filling space. Waffle gives rhetoric a bad name."

"Quite", said Pat minimally.

I woke up. And thought: now I know how to begin Chapter One.

I think what I'm going to be saying, again and again, in different forms, is that communication is glory, and vice versa, and that the essence of communication is the glorious taking of risks. That goes for God as well as for us. Communication which makes any effort to connect with the divine is going to be more than minimalist. It isn't, on the other hand, going to inflate into empty waffle. What it is going to do is push the boat out. When God created the cosmos, a pretty big boat was being pushed. The Big Bang was hardly a minimalist gesture. Whether or not you go along with Stephen Hawking's deconstruction of eternity, the universe we now inhabit is not just star-studded and crammed with purple passages (sunsets were appearing before the first Hollywood film or pulpit prayer). It is massively complex and still bursting with evolutionary potential.

If God is mixed up in all this, is communication the same as communion? Yes, I think so. Maybe communication is communion being busy: evolving, stretching. Sometimes, too busy? Then we need the silence. A subliminal text can come through a silence. But also, an inner silence can come through the most riotous physical noise. Whether you call it Art or Religion or God, or just being intensely alive, that is the glory of high communication: the dangerously risky moment, in which dimensions overlap.

Trapped the other day without a book in a train which had lost the will to move, I worked out that I'd written something like eight million words in my adult life, and that's not including memos. What for? The articles, papers, editorials, scripts, sermons, prayers, talks, letters, do not survive. What was the point? I suppose they were just me saying: "Here I am.

There you are. And somewhere in and around and between us is significance." Either that significance got communicated at the time or it didn't.

But the possibility that there might be communication, that is the glory; even if one's best efforts remain sketches. We can all understand the frustration of Arthur Sullivan's fabled organist with the chord fetish, groping for his perfect amen. The spirit of delight may come rarely; perfection never. On earth, dead butterflies do not fly, and information on what goes on in heaven is not available. But true communication hints at absolutes and can suggest perfection. Moreover, it doesn't always come via the great writers or composers. A gem of naïve honesty can strike a chord so clear that a miniature moment can be transfigured. That is why a hymn thought little of by the musical establishment may reach parts that approved hymns don't reach. And that's why I've heard encores by great visiting orchestras from America and Russia unman an audience in a way the preceding symphonic performances didn't. Not because the encores were tuneful, famous, and brief - audiences are more sophisticated these days and don't need bribing by lollipops - but because the 'work' of the evening accomplished, the players and conductor were letting their hair down, allowing their hearts to speak, and that was going straight to the audience's heart. At such moments I've felt myself surrounded by an attention so rapt it was like being a child again on Christmas Eve. Emotional? Yes, exactly.

Whether we're talking about an orchestra, a hymn, a sermon, a prayer, organ voluntary, solo song, we're talking about the human drive to communicate which can reflect and include God. There is an inside and an outside to this. The inside is the logic, the structure, the grammar - the bones. The outside is the performance, the impression - the skin.

Let me describe a specific encore which will reinforce points I'm making elsewhere about speeds, loudness and the taking of risks, but which will here underline the distinction I'm drawing between structure and performance. By an odd chance I was able to compare two performances of the identical encore given by the same orchestra and conductor. In November 1991, the St. Petersburg Philharmonic with its conductor Yuri Temirkanov gave two concerts to capacity audiences in Glasgow's Royal Concert Hall. Temirkanov doesn't wear his heart on his sleeve. He wears it, in the form of a large white handkerchief, in his breast pocket. From there it emerges for the theatrical removal of moisture surplus to requirements. By the time we reached the first encore we were all as exhausted as he had made quite clear he was. Then the magic. It was the *pas de deux* from the Nutcracker Suite. If you analyse it, the theme is little more than a downward scale. The speed at which he took it was as dangerously slow as the Bernstein 'Nimrod' I describe later. It could hardly be danced at that speed. He also maximised the dynamic range from extreme pianissimo to veryloudindeedissimo. It slew us. And I mean that respectfully. I couldn't forget it for weeks. I still haven't forgotten it.

Nine months later I happened to tune in to the conclusion of a live Prom on BBC TV. Same orchestra, same Yuri (there are two conducting Yuris). Same encore. Different encore. Same notes, different event in space-time. Same structure, totally different emotional reality.

The obvious difference lay in the speed which was more normal. It was a standard performance by a fine orchestra. With the (musically dubious) assistance of camera close-ups, one could tell the conductor was literally going through the motions - in his case still considerable motions. The players didn't seem particularly *engagé*. That I confess to be a highly fallible impression, but I won't budge from asserting that there was a major gap in overall voltage. Why?

There could be a hundred reasons, as many as there are individual lives in an orchestra. But an obvious explanation is at hand. At the Glasgow concert in November, the Moscow coup was but three months past, and Yeltsin still in a power struggle with Gorbachev. The Soviet Union was disintegrating and Mother Russia was suffering a winter of grave food shortages. The city from which the players came had only just changed its name - my tickets were marked 'Leningrad Philharmonic' - and ex-colleagues of mine were meeting the orchestra and processing relief supplies. Audience and orchestra were bonded in a sense of deep familial concern. It was, in short, a liturgical moment, and music of great simplicity spoke to that moment. It was a prayer.

There is a place for bare logic - but it is not in music, certainly not religious music. No, not even in Bach. As we'll see later, classical counterpoint is not clockwork, nor for that matter is bare plainsong. If all you see is bones, something is not well. The images of Belsen, Somalia, the Balkans, disturb because they reflect people who are dying. But the converse is true. Shelley, Blake, Chaikovsky, George Matheson - are not just romantic wafflers squeezing out shapeless purple passages. Under the shining skin is a bony structure, a climbing frame for blossom. There are, of course, different kinds of structure. That of the semi-operatic nineteenth century hymn may seem different from that of the sinewy sixteenth century psalm tune, and both may differ from that of a twentieth century song. Yet their inner structures are close. It is the colour and fragrance of their surface that is different, and there should be no problem at all in enjoying all of them.

I was taught both verbal and musical grammar by inspired teachers, and whether I'm writing non-minimalist prose or improvising impressionistic noises on piano or organ, I have relied (successfully or otherwise) on these structures I inherited. You only can push the boat out if you have a boat to push. The first *sine qua non* is some kind of sound craft. What I want to suggest in these lectures is that soundness is not always what it is thought to be. Soundness is not always good taste or conventional competence or fashionable approval. Throughout our churches and communities there exist a multitude of crafts. They may be of all sizes, speeds, and abilities, like the variety of crafts which crossed the channel in 1940 to rescue the British Army from the Dunkirk beaches, but, like that uneven flotilla, they can do the job: in this case the job of saving that wonderful communicative glory: the churches' song.

So where do we begin? With passion. In all their variety, the boats got to Dunkirk and back with a disciplined commitment - the rational element; but also with an undertow of urgency, danger, suffering - elements of high drama. Without vision, the people perish; without passion, music is dead on the page. Passion, however, is more than feeling... and more than rationality. It is the fibre made by the entwining of both. Music which matters is a struggle to batter through a sea of feelings with a solid craft - however small - which can be rationally steered.

I am fortunate enough to be a member of the West Kirk in Helensburgh, where the music maker is Walter Blair, Director of the Junior School at the Royal Scottish Academy of Music. He has been organist at the West Kirk for twenty-eight years, which says something about his commitment. But what about staleness? Ah, there might be the rub. Might be. But isn't. Each Sunday, the project of lifting the worship is approached with passion. I think I can detect the odd Sunday when he is not genuinely inspired. But even then, one is excited, because the fibre of his commitment brings him and us onto a high level of engaged seriousness. He never fails to attack - organ, hymns, anthem, the lot. Discipline, you see, is not a boringly rational factor. Discipline is cousin to discipleship. And that, as you will recall, was intimately connected with passion.

OK, we can't all be Walter Blair. But I have been moved in many a country or small town church over the years by an organist of limited ability who has with passion led the hymns in such a way as to lift the congregation's understanding. And what of those of us who are not practising musicians of any kind? We all have to live day by day, and music can be a passion at the heart of our lives.

It is not given to many to be organists, pulpit stars, or poets. Few become architects or generals. Not a lot of us make it to be designers of clothes or aircraft. Only a tiny minority become even flyers of aircraft. Most of us do not see what we think are visions. And yet.

And yet we are immortal. Or have intimations of immortality. We drink of life. Like Christ, we suffer and laugh. (It was

G.K.Chesterton who ventured the enlivening thought that
when Jesus went away to be alone it was to laugh. I like that
picture. Splitting, so to speak, his sides in an agony of hilarity
at the lunacies that had encompassed his day; but too sensitive
to have hurt feelings by relieving the pressure on his funny-
bone in front of vulnerable souls. Of course, He cried too. The
two kinds of tears are close.)

Like him, like everyone, we have these moments of enhanced awareness. The helpless giggle over a banana skin. The
taking in of breath at a puppy tumbling, a wagtail bouncing
across a lawn, a toddler running to its mother. Or, at the dark
end of the spectrum, the face of a starving child, or a old man
dying, coming at us out of the TV screen, haunting us with its
implacable declaration of mortality. At such moments, we
connect with something wider than job, comfort, convenience.
But really it is there all the time: the stab of momentary
awareness of an alternative dimension; in the loved voice,
lapping waves, autumn wind, winter storm, beautiful woman,
distant train, noise of the city at night, church bells... and the
moments of terror in danger, lonely freedom, exposed decision-
making.

Which is what this book is about. It is about hearing tunes.
Tunes of glory. Tunes of reality. Singing them, or playing them,
but in the first instance hearing them, because we can all do that.
It is about hearing tunes in life, in one's head, through one's ears
- the inner one as well as the outer one.

The immortality which can be touched by tunes is available
in church and out. But since these thoughts originated in
lectures about music and God, I'm particularly concerned to
say that tunes - glorious tunes - can still actually be heard in
church. Yes - in church! All the talk about church music being
boring, or having become boring is loose talk. The rumours
about church music being dead or dying are - well, just that, idle
gossip. Reports of the decease of church music have been greatly
exaggerated. It just isn't so. Nor need it be so.

We should neither believe melancholy old organists and
ministers who say the best lies behind us, and ahead stretches a

trackless desert of mindless mediocrity; nor should we give credence to excitable new wave young (or acting young) musicians and clergy who, dismissing the past, say the best is all ahead, and, go ahead, folks, CLAP!

Skippers of sound craft, however modest, have a more balanced approach. Even if they are not steering by the stars, their compasses and radar are not dictated to by passing moods and fashions. Not only musicians and clergy, but the majority who are neither, would probably think that by definition the best so far is in the past, but that by the same historical definition, if one has any faith at all, an even greater amount of the best lies in the future. The best, in other words, is potentially everywhere. But it has to be navigated now.

In considering what sometimes appears to be a dialogue of the deaf on these matters, should we perhaps tackle the linguistic obstacles presented by the very existence of the words 'best' and 'past'?

'THE BEST'

What should church music aim at, in any age, in any circumstance? The best! Of course. Naturally. What else, when God is involved?

But what is the best? How do you recognise it, let alone achieve it?

More fundamentally: is there such a thing? Does 'the best' exist?

Even in religious communities, is an ideal 'best' a chimera? In the late nineteen sixties, as Executive Producer of 50% of ITV's network religious output from London, I was much exercised by such questions. Quality control, an industrial concept, was central to an industry like ITV, where the product had to sell to advertisers *via* viewers, but quality of what? That was a riddle religious TV had to grapple with, for was not God about something more than saleability? (A conundrum pressing even more sharply today as cable and satellite options proliferate in the market.)

I received a startlingly simple insight on this matter in the less than obvious venue of Windsor Castle. The then Dean of

Windsor was minded from time to time to summon sundry great and good to mingle there with a number of those still toiling at the rockface of this or that field of endeavour. As a reward for brain-thrashing and think-tanking one's way through a number of seminars, one enjoyed the *frisson* of resting one's bones on a Windsor bed. This weekend, it was a media, society, and industry work-out in which journalists, editors, generals, producers and knights of industry hammered away at social values. One of the speakers was the Chairman of Courtaulds, and he sliced the ceiling off my brain when he said, "The best is the enemy of the good."

Not a new thought. But the success of this industrialist carried weight. In essence he was saying: if your activity is directed obsessively at an unattainable standard, you may fail to achieve what is attainable. If you insist on brilliance, you may impede merit. Don't let an ideal aim distract you from an achievable one.

Buried within that truism is a message of great practical importance: that we should not be hypnotised by 'standards'. All too often, a 'standard' means a standardisation; and all too often that means standing at the station, stationary, with no motive power to take an enterprise further along the line of the possible.

The fact is, of course, that 'the best' is as relative a term as 'good'. What is objectively valuable, or subjectively valued, varies from place to place as much as from time to time. In Chapter Six, I consider the whole question of objective and subjective values. For the moment I only wish to underline that no worshipping group anywhere should feel under pressure to achieve music-making for which it lacks either the heart or the ability; nor should any musician feel intimidated into aiming for a best which is so wildly unrealistic that aiming for it produces a worst. But that doesn't mean being cowed into the opposite, a nervous acceptance of the dull and safe. One intimidation is as bad as the other. The true value is freedom. Where there is a freedom - and that is a fundamental Christian category - to be as modest or outrageous as may be, free to be unapologetically traditional here and dangerously experimental there, then there will be life; and that will be the actual best. Not a safe 'standard', not a stereotypical standardisation, either ancient or modern, but a happening in the here and now, which lifts these people at this moment into a space where liberty of mind or head or body is experienced, or all of these, or permutations of these.

'THE PAST'

For church music, the past is an irrelevant concept. It always was, for what an absurd misconception it would be to think that against the ticking of the cosmic clock an idea, a tune, or style in, say 1789, was automatically inferior to its counterpoint in 1889. Rather the reverse, some would say - and they would be wrong also. Yet this chronological snake still hypnotises us. Many do assume that the product of 1989 must be better than that of 1889. Or, if not better in an absolute sense, then more relevant, more useful. That is what I dispute. On the snakes and ladders board of church music, the snake is the concept of time past and the ladders are the rigid structures of current fashion.

Worship is more like chess: a multidimensional game where every piece (every worshipper) has her or his role to play; where freedom counterpoints within the discipline of complex rules across space and time, and where the outcome is never predictable. This multidimensional framework harmonises with what we are discovering about the dynamic relativities of space-time in the structure of the cosmos, not to mention the layers of conceptual rigidity being stripped away by voyagers into the worlds of quantum, chaos and sub-particle worlds whose technical terms seem to lose shelf-life from month to month.

So let no organist, choirmaster, minister or priest be blackmailed by the imagined past ('it's aye bin like that'), or an imagined present or future fashion ('unless you do this, we won't get the young folk in'). If all we get the young folk into is a charnel house of contemporary dry bones, why bother?

Having thrown out these preliminary questions, and before trying to engage with them at length, I'd like to encapsulate the main burden of what I've been trying to say so far in one story.

The story centres on a grey old building which broods, sometimes it seems morosely, on a ridge of Auld Reekie. Nudged by lawyers, councillors, and the patrons of howffs, and infested in summer by camera-bearing Belgians, you can see it through an outsider's eyes as (a) a mausoleum of long ago events, (b) a tourist attraction, (c) a cheap lunch in the crypt, (d) a highbrow sort of place for Sunday worship.

I saw it as an insider. I choose St. Giles Cathedral at this point because it represents Presbyterianism. Maybe that doesn't matter any more. Or maybe it does. For out of the maw of the Reformation faith there issues this rock-hard challenge: can the word as reality be encountered again and again in our time? The Kirk of Scotland, like the Church of England, is an established church. Like it or not, it is there to serve the whole people. St. Giles was at one time the epicentre of national revolution. Evolution is more our way now - and just by walking into St. Giles you can see the visual marks of liturgical evolution. It is, however, a musical story I have to tell, for one of my messages is that 'the word' is not about words.

The Queen was in town... Not for the first time, you might say, knowing the town. Ah, that's where you'd be wrong. It was the first time. It had been a year of heightened British consciousness (the movement towards Scottish consciousness showing only fitful political signs). The King had died. Hillary's British team had climbed Everest, then far from being the busy tourist destination it is now. The young Elizabeth had been televised to the nation from Westminster Abbey. And now crowned, she had come across the border; her mission to engage in an act of commitment to the Scottish people. And where else to do that but in the High Kirk of Edinburgh. There, if in any one church building, that Kirk was forged which the new Queen was pledged to defend.

It was half past eleven on the night before the service, and, apart from a handful of security men, I was alone in St. Giles.

Earlier, the building had been flooded with light for final camera rehearsals, the walls had been awash with organ music, the rafters ringing with the sound of choristers, and the old flags shivering to brass fanfares. I suppose the flags hadn't really shivered, but my spine had. I was then assistant organist to Herrick Bunney and I was involved in this glorious mayhem up to the hilt. I was still young enough (three and a half decades before scientists floated the chaos theory into public consciousness), to perceive intuitively that the more minute your planning, the nearer you get to the anarchy at the heart of existence. (Young people and very old people know this. The middle-aged keep it at bay.)

Charles Warr, the small but perfectly formed Dean of the Thistle, had mapped out the entire service with a meticulous care honed by a lifetime of ecclesiastical flummery. He was indulgent to me, as an insignificant whippersnapper, just one tiny cog in the elaborate liturgical machine assembled for the event. Another mogul was equally indulgent: Ronald Falconer, then in charge of Scotland's BBC religious broadcasting. A crisp moustachioed man, of an avuncular jollity masking a steely command of his fiefdom, he commissioned me, at one camera rehearsal of a procession, to come out of the organ loft and take the place of the Lord Lyon, King of Arms. This was the nearest I ever got to being a Colossus on the world stage. I mimed the then elderly Lord Lyon's disjunctive lope - totter would be within an inch of exaggeration - to such effect that Ronnie Falconer dined out on it for weeks.

All this had been highly amusing. But it had vanished like melting ice-cream. What I was now confronted with was reality. An empty St. Giles. Richard Dimbleby, the commentator, had gone off to his hotel. The camera crews were in their beds or their pubs. Clergy, civil servants, royal advisers were with their wives or their whisky. The choirs, trumpets, trombonists, and drummers were wherever. Here I was in a vast and shadowy space, alone with an organ console; and in dialogue with the hard core of a worship challenge I could not escape.

To describe this challenge, I have to introduce the only mogul that mattered to me at that moment, Herrick Bunney. Later I will have many things to say about this remarkable man.

His significance for me at this moment was that he had done something absolutely staggering. A couple of days before, he had entrusted me with the climax of the service. Apart from all the visual glory - the brilliance of the lights, processions, colours, robes, uniforms - it was to be a journey round a pantheon of high musical moments. Everything was timed to the second, and from the moment an hour before the service that the first voluntary began, the experience would roll towards glory - or, inconceivably, disaster. Nothing was left to chance. My spine still tingles when I recall Herrick's beginning that inexorable process by bringing his hands down at the split second on the first chord of the noble Elgar Organ Sonata. That was the beginning. What of the end?

After the Queen had received the Honours of Scotland - crown, sceptre, and so on - before the communion table, she was to turn and process out. Herrick chose me, a musical child, to be the father of that climactic moment. It is only looking back from the vantage point of maturity that I now realise what an act of courage and faith that was. What he said was: improvise. *Improvise*: on the air, on TV, on film, before all the ermined and medallioned great and good of Scotland: *improvise?*

His musical rationale was this: over the previous two hours and more he would have been flooding the old stone walls and the airwaves with everything he could prepare: organ, brass fanfares, choral climaxes, congregational shouts, all conceived, designed, rehearsed, refined, as only Herrick Bunney could, and then blooming into a thousand musical colours as only he could make them flower. But at this moment, he wanted something different. So he said, "Go for broke. Don't play safe. Jump off the cliff. Crash in against the dying chords of the brass fanfare. Let the moment carry you." These may not have been the exact words, but it was certainly the message.

What nerve, what generosity, what trust! It wasn't as if he couldn't improvise. He has always been a master of the inspired processional paean. It was as if Gary Lineker sent himself off the field in injury time. And what a hair-raising risk! At that moment I could have destroyed everything that he had built up. He almost lost his nerve when the night before I'd told him I planned to improvise on the theme, 'She'll be coming round the mountain when she comes'. But he trusted me to be joking. And I repaid that trust by trusting in his faith that I could somehow do it - but, I now see, it was not me he was trusting. It was the moment. He was trusting that God would be in that moment. He was trusting that if we stepped off the cliff together, with the danger of musical and professional death, something real would be born. So was it? Was it real? Or was it in the event, just musical waffle? I can't tell you. That's the point. It was, at that moment, 'the word'. Or wasn't. Whether it was is a secret of history, known only to people long gone, or to minds which will not remember.

But how moving to listen, four decades later, to the recent Radio Scotland programme when we heard the actual sounds of that great old organ, not only dying but being killed. Dismantled. Pipe after pipe, cable after cable, taken down, taken away. A creature of once golden glory returning to dust.

So that a new creature might arise to lead in the praise of glory.

Later in the programme we heard the glory of the same Herrick Bunney playing the new organ, now one of the finest anywhere. He and the organ I'd once played had grown old together. He and the reborn organ were young again. On eagle's wings indeed. But then Herrick's own wings have always been in working order. He has always been willing to risk the moment.

Life and death are paradoxical, beyond our comprehension; and round the paradoxes may cluster pain of the deepest red. But if you trust the risky moment, from the ground of God there may blossom, to beyond the stars, life that shall endless be.

Chapter Two

THE GOLDEN MEAN

A friend - at least I think he is - referred to this book as a prospective exercise in "*Kirche und Kitsch*" - roughly translatable as the church and bad taste. It was a gauntlet teasingly thrown down. I am more than happy to pick it up and to wrap it tenderly around everything I have to say. Because if we are afraid of bad taste, we are afraid to live, let alone worship. If we are afraid to make mistakes, afraid of judgement by professional or peer groups, afraid of philistinism, afraid of being caught out, we will be so paralysed by the glare from all those imagined (or actual) judgements that, like a rabbit transfixed by car headlights, we will die of immobility. Conscious or unconscious fear is, I suspect, one of the root causes of the apparent *malaise* of much of our church music in Scotland: the endemic Scottish fear of being caught out, caught at it, caught being vulnerable, caught being wrong.

An underlying theme that I think will be heard running through nearly every story I tell will be the central role of personal experience. The answer to whatever problems there are in church music lies mainly within each of us. It is not always extra financial resources that are required, though they are helpful. It is not a sudden new surge of professional musicians that will save us; that would be wonderful, but it simply isn't available. It is not new organs, new groups, or a revolution in choral techniques that will determine the future of song in the church. It is not even new songs, reinvigorating though they are. It is the exercise of our imaginations and the activity of our emotions that will decide whether magic returns to church music - if, indeed, it is missing. But counterpointing that personal theme is a counter-subject of depth and difficulty.

We have to begin by understanding what music is about. And why it costs so much effort. And why it is worth the effort: of composing it, performing it, listening to it. It is about death. That is why it costs so much. And that is why it is worth more than its weight in gold.

A son going off, to university, job, or war, that is a death to those who are left behind, and it may be a death for him, too. A daughter going off to career, college, marriage; that is a death to her family; and something inside her may die. Something that has to die, for her to evolve. Built into the normal universal rhythm of human life is this dying, this wrenching, this pain. And I haven't mentioned illness, hospital, divorce, bereavement, or any of the other disasters that flesh is heir to. I'm talking about events that involve the discord of emotional pain and that psychic disjunction which is necessary for spiritual growth... one is saying no more than has been said by spiritual gurus down the ages, as when Jesus talked about the need for seed to fall into the ground if there is to be new growth: if, to paraphrase George Matheson's famous lines, there is to blossom, from the ground of being, new being. For - of course - these common human dyings are rich in potential resurrections. Out of the living cathedrals of marriage, or work, or out of solitariness built lonely stone by painful stone in the lives of those who do not find expanding structures to live in, out of all human experience, is born again the Son of Man, who comes again and again on clouds of glory. Whether these clouds are dark ones with silver linings or gold ones with dark linings is impossible to disentangle. Good Friday and Easter, Christmas and Pentecost, are intertwined in the one fiery ball of experience. The joy in life's pain and the ache in life's joys, are the twin progeny of being alive: and they are at the heart of music.

Music involves three things: phenomenal attention to the detail of sound patterns; conceptual architecture in an infinite perspective; and a commingling of pain and delight. The pain and delight proceed from the tension between detail and infinity. Because the universe is not a straight line, but a golden ball, disintegrating, exploding, expanding, evolving, re-integrating, the detail and the infinite come round in the dance of meaning to face each other in struggle and embrace. You see it in the Epstein sculpture of Jacob wrestling with the angel. The classic musical microcosm of this struggle is the discord. The macrocosm you see classically in the structures of fugue, sonata, symphony, opera. Try to imagine a fugue without discord, a symphony without conflict, an opera without a catalytic crisis. You cannot do it. You cannot separate form and essence. The concepts fall apart. But also: try to imagine the New Testament without the crucifixion. The fact that I can add that without obviously changing key is significant. It explains why not only in medieval, classical, or Victorian times did composers find Christian ideas compatible, indeed inspirational, but in our secular age as well. This compatibility between musical discord and conflict on the one hand and Christian theology on the other, provides a key to evaluating much simpler musical artefacts than symphonies and operas, namely hymns.

What is a hymn? It is a bridge between on the one hand that infinite attention to the most intricate detail which is the work of the professional musician, whether composer, performer or analyst, and on the other hand, that simplicity which gives music its *raison d'être* in the spiritual Pantheon. There are many topics one could cover in a survey of church music: enough for a hundred lectures. But, just as I rejected the use of visual and audio equipment to enrich the fabric of the lectures, because I thought it misleading to play in at the press of a button, choirs, orchestra, organ, and congregations beyond the reach of the average church, so I have rejected covering so much ground at a height of 30,000 feet that one is by the end not conscious of having made a real journey and seen the actual terrain.

What are the main ingredients of the environment in which most people of the ground experience church music? They are, still, in the congregational scene, the basic instrument - usually the organ to which I will refer particularly later, the choir; and the congregation. And what is it that these will most commonly do? Why, sing hymns. My contention is that if we get the hymns right, we have every chance of getting everything else right. This is more obviously true in the hymn sandwich liturgy of the Church of Scotland and other related Reformed traditions, but I would argue that it holds for nearly all Western Christian forms of service. I have taken part in Anglican and Roman Catholic cathedral celebrations based on choir-led orders, which would have not fulfilled their spiritual remits if a couple of hymns had not, at critical moments, gathered the detail and the infinite together in a simple but sweeping architectural span. At these moments, the golden ball of the Christian cosmos is gathered together out of the disparate elements of a dozen, or a hundred, or a thousand human lives and thrown into the air; for one of the perpetual challenges of the hymn is that its performance is unpredictable.

There are so many random factors waiting to work every time a hymn is announced that the organist playing over the first line is just as heroically about to step off the cliff as a conductor stepping on to the platform to face an unfamiliar orchestra. The difference is that some organists are not as aware of this as they might be. I will, therefore, refer to hymns as significant, both for the practical reason I have just outlined that they constitute the liturgical fulcrum of our common worship; but also because they provide a touchstone of the values implicit in the way we approach church music in general. Of course, one can get the hymns right, and other things wrong; but it is less likely that one will get other musical matters right if one treats the hymns wrong - for example, casually, contemptuously, boringly, unrhythmically, or without sensitivity to the words. On the other hand, it is possible to treat hymns with a mind-numbing degree of vulgar melodrama. Not that vulgarity is by definition to be excluded. The right kind of vulgarity is as valid an ingredient in the worship cocktail as, in its time, was the Latin Vulgate; and if one suggests, as I will, that God, judging by the evidence, is a Great Entertainer, then an element of *kitsch*, of bad taste, is as entitled to feel at home in the range of liturgical entertainment as a Norman pillar or a baroque ceiling. Indeed, it sometimes needs a tourist better educated than I am to assess what in a baroque church in Central Europe is *kitsch* and what is high art. When, for example, is a nativity tableau charming *kitsch*, when is it art, and when is it just embarrassing?

Recently I visited the Church of Holy Mary, Mother of All Angels, adjoining Prague Castle. In a kind of crypt, there is a nativity tableau of breath-taking boldness. Its depth is greater than its width. You stand with the life-size shepherds and their sheepdog behind you, and in front the scene round the crib, the Magi opulent with their *entourage*, and away beyond them, fading into an actual physical distance like the farthest point on a deep opera stage, a golden city set on a hill, which I found to be remarkably evocative of the real Bethlehem when I visited Israel later in the making of the same film. Lying beside the crib in Prague are two lambs. At the toss of a coin into a hat, one lamb opens a mouth and goes "Baa", the other one opens its mouth and responds "Baa". This has to be *kitsch*. Yet the whole scene has such power that it somehow carries the absurdity past one's sense of the ridiculous into the heart. This room is opened for two weeks every Christmas, and the queue stretches miles down the hill. How dare people be so fond of *kitsch*? The question is, of course, begged. One man's bad taste is another gentleman's relish.

Showing us this Nativity tableau was a Capuchin monk. The church was attached to a monastery, but he was the only monk left. In the Stalinist days, the monastery was an army barracks, and Brother Mark, like the others, was put in prison merely for being a monk. Now, his brown habit restored to him, he looked after the church. He was old and bent, with a face in repose of appalling humility - appalling in its exposure of one's own egocentricity - but, his smile of rapture at the treasures in his care was carefree. I asked him through the interpreter if he felt any particular carol suited the scene. He answered in Czech through the interpreter, a ball of energy named Dasa, 'From The Heart Of Mary, A Flower Is Born'. I asked, "Could either of you sing it?" They both did. The monk began, tremulously, his recently imprisoned voice speaking like a broken reed in an organ abandoned on a scrap heap. Dasa joined in, and their voices gained confidence. I pause here to remind you: they were singing in a tiny space between a group of large shepherds plus collie dog, a phalanx of wise men, one of whom looked like Othello, and a Channel Four film crew. It was as if we were in the middle of a Bill Bryden miracle play in the Cottesloe Theatre crossed with a Citizen's Theatre Christmas pantomime, and suddenly transposed to the Jorvik Viking Centre in York. It was away beyond being a matter of taste, good or bad. It was like that moment just beyond the point of no return when an aircraft has to rise into the sky or die, and has begun to drum your ears into the back of your seat with the effort to be airborne - and then suddenly is. In the midst of the absurdity, what the monk and the interpreter were singing was a chorale-like carol. The two inadequate voices blended in a rising tide of conviction - one Catholic monk, one Protestant woman, singing to a British TV production unit.

Our producer was not in that room. He was in the adjoining church, puzzled and moved by the distant effect of the *a cappella* sound. The rest of us joined him, and asked the monk about his story, one of patient suffering, which he wore lightly. We already knew Dasa's story, which has culminated in her being possibly Prague's top interpreter who interprets for her hero, the playwright turned president, Vaclav Havel. Ray, the producer, asked if I'd like to play the baroque organ, high in the gallery. I played three things - 'Adeste Fideles', 'Hark the Herald Angels Sing', and an improvised toccata. The instrument had that French brilliance which verges on out-of-tuneness. The carols sparked into the ancient church like a display of firecrackers. The monk approached and spread before me some music. It was the carol he and Dasa had sung. As I played it, he knelt and prayed, and my colleagues down in the church saw his face transfigured. The House of God which had been raped, pillaged and sold for thirty pieces of Marxist dogma, had today breathed, sung and been *kitsched* - kissed - into life. No less a commitment should we make with every hymn we sing. If we are afraid of hymns taking off into raw emotion, then we should avoid them altogether.

I said at the outset that music is about death, or to put it musically, discord. This is, I believe, a true statement, but not an obviously true one. In the case of Christian music, I would hold it to be self-evidently true. The child in the crib did not only die, as all babies die by the time they are thirty, seventy or a hundred. The baby in the crib died in a form which was defined as crucial. The monk who sang that carol had once died: he had ceased to be a monk. The lady who interpreted had lived through two deaths of freedom in her beloved Czechoslovakia. Our driver had seen friends die in 1968. The church and monastery of Holy Mary had died. Now they had all experienced a resurrecting hope; and Dasa worked with a man she described as the Word made Flesh: a playwright president, who had been imprisoned for the sake of his words, and had now with healing words set the captive free. You cannot have Christmas without Good Friday, and neither Christmas, nor Good Friday ring bells in infinity without Easter Sunday.

I have told that story for all sorts of reasons, which will unfold, but let me underline a musical point. It is not only a pious dominical truism that where two or three are gathered together, something may happen; it is a musical truth. In this case what were the elements of sound that made up a powerful emotional cocktail? Two artificial lambs going baa; two unimpressive voices singing a Medieval carol; and an organ playing some Victorian carols. Admittedly, the visual environment was strong, but the atmosphere in many a plain church can be just as strong when you step in off the street.

It is not what big extra musical resources you can get that matters, it is what you do emotionally with the resources you have. You may be familiar with that proposition of the new science which has already achieved the status of a platitude in stating that the flapping of butterflies' wings in the Amazonian jungle may cause a tornado in Texas. Using this as an image and not as a proof, I would suggest that the way we deal with the second hymn at the morning service in the Old Parish Church of Muckleshuggle on a Sunday morning in bleakest February, may determine whether bells ring out across the cosmos, a million starfields from now. If you don't accept that connection, then singing in church is probably a rather out of date form of communal vocal therapy. Infinitesimal detail and infinity are mutually incarnate whenever a soul takes off at the end of the runway of emotional and intellectual risk. Music is one of the human runways which faces clearly into the prevailing wind of death. A hymn, at its best, adds the engine of artistic integrity to the wings of spiritual *naïveté*. If it all works, you have lift off.

I will try to be spare in the adumbration of doctrine. This is partly because of a reluctance to pinion the butterfly of spontaneity on the page of principle, and partly because principles, grandiose though they may sound when couched in professional jargon, usually boil down to common sense. But every now and then it may be helpful to floodlight a piece of common sense, so here is a nostrum: the detail must be carried by the whole.

Let me rephrase that in various ways: the whole must be strong enough to bear a strongly emphasised detail. The nativity scene must be powerful enough to carry baaing lambs. By all means make a dramatic point, but only if you can do so without fatally damaging the dramatic impulse of the whole. A decorative detail must not spoil the architectural sweep. To put it more boldly, if a hymn tune is worth doing at all, it is worth taking the risk of doing badly. For the sake of making a dramatic point, you may have to risk miscalculating and spoiling the whole effect. Some great cathedrals have gargoyles, where the masons let their hair down and fashioned faces which would send Monty Python and Spitting Image artists running to Mummy. But they were usually put in positions where they do not threaten the composure of the whole perspective, in other words, where they are invisible. That is a relatively safe process. In other cathedrals, you may find a feature which you suspect has taken the more serious risk of spoiling the overall perspective - for example, an organ screen impeding the flow from nave to choir. But, short of taking it down, you can't be sure. That syncopation in the overall rhythm may be just what the building needs to avoid a relentless drive of the eye to a second-rate reredos at the east end. It all comes down to balance, some sort of golden mean. But I must flesh out this simple principle with examples, so let us for the time being leave the worlds of hymn singing and architecture and attend to the methods of very great music makers.

Sir Adrian Boult was the most architectural of conductors. This wasn't accidental. He intended to be so: it was a conscious approach. He articulated it in a simple way. In any given concert there should be one main climax, and all other climaxes should be graded down from that. Within each work the same control of emotional contour applied: one Ben Nevis, other lesser Munros, and then hills and hillocks. This intelligent appraisal of the decibelic landscape was implicit in his style of conducting. Those who like the conductor to be a balletic visual aid to the music drama found Boult dull. He just stood there, a moustachioed colonel of the regiment, beating time for the officers and other ranks. Ah, but if you got close enough to see how he beat time, and if you listened! His control of the baton was legendary. It was a long baton, and he was able to flick his wrist in a way which made its point go into a minuscule spasm which communicated across the orchestra. For a bigger effect he might jerk the whole stick. For a dramatic effect he might move the lower arm slightly across his body. And if he wished to unleash a fortissimo he indulged himself to the terrifying extent of raising his arm somewhat and then lowering it with a final whiplash of the wrist. This was indeed fine motor control in the service of a balance between detail and overall perspective. I recall, with affection, three particular examples of how effective this was. The first was in what you might call a routine performance of Mendelssohn's music from 'A Midsummer Night's Dream'. In the scherzo there is a sequence in three time when the first note in every six is lightly accented, but the first note in every twenty-four accentuated slightly more. I watched every time that accent was reached. Not only did the wrist flick, but the whole arm shot slightly forward. This sent a tremor through the orchestra, and a tiny magic chuckle animated Mendelssohn's melodic line. I have watched other more dynamic conductors doing this piece, and either that moment passes unnoticed, or the accent is too crudely ostentatious.

Not long before fire destroyed the St. Andrews Halls in Glasgow, I heard Boult conduct Vaughan Williams' 'London Symphony'. I had heard it the night before in Edinburgh, and had found it so magical, I took the train through to Glasgow to hear it again. I can still hear the symphony's opening and its closing epilogue as they were that night. Boult stood emotionally as impassive as the Cenotaph, brooding over Whitehall. His hand and baton hardly moved. The strings were so hushed they appeared to disappear. The symphony moves from London at dawn through a day of busily changing moods to the magic moment of the great city wrapping itself again in sleep. Out of the palpable dark float the distant chimes of Big Ben. In the haunting acoustic of that old hall, it was a remote bell tolling in a child's dream of long long ago. Why was it OK to have Big Ben chiming in a symphony? In what way is this less *kitsch* than lambs baaing? Because, as with the cuckoo in Delius's 'On Hearing The First Cuckoo In Spring', the sound is not thrust at you ostentatiously. Its *naïveté* is cradled tenderly in an atmospheric texture woven with sophisticated craftsmanship. And Boult's conducting was so gossamer, he spun the web so delicately, that there was an extra courtesy of space and distance, as in a cathedral, so that one did not feel pressurised to make a judgement. But quiet magic was not Boult's only trick. Years later, I attended a performance of 'Belshazzar's Feast' at the Royal Festival Hall. Behind my wife and me were music students from the Royal College of Music. The programme note told us that the dynamic young conductor we'd expected was sick, and Sir Adrian had taken his place at short notice. The students were disappointed and scathing. They thought, and in the way of students, did not hesitate to say loudly for the benefit of the rest of us, that even in his prime, Boult was the only conductor who could rob Walton's music of its pagan ferocity. Now, in his geriatricity, he would kill it. I wasn't so sure, but I recognised there might be a mismatch between a fastidious and now frail English gentleman and Walton's muscular material. I needn't have doubted. For if your control is based not on the acrobatics of adolescence or the physical drive of early manhood, but on intelligence, age is not a handicap. It was an electrifying performance. The old wrist flicked to startling effect. The lower arm swept the choir into thrilling climaxes. At the peroration, the whole arm raised itself in judgement, then crashed on the rostrum rail, and the choir jumped. At the end the students were dumbfounded. "My God," said one, "the old boy pulled that off." Yes, my God, I thought, he did, didn't he, you pompous little git. You see, colonels of the regiment have their passions. They have, however, learned to channel them. The same is true of good organists leading good hymns.

The principle of balance between detail and total effect is even more important for organists than for conductors. What is the image of the conductor? A man of power, I guess. I don't think this is entirely due to the ancient status handicap shared by a male dominated career in holy orders. The drive to dominate in a physical way was built into the role of the modern conductor as it developed in the heyday of the nineteenth Century romantic orchestra, where the impression is that the conductor is controlling and unleashing vast forces. But think about it. The conductor is actually in possession of no power whatsoever. It is all, literally, sleight of hand. He is faced with a band of musicians who, if they so choose can reduce him in a matter of minutes to utter helplessness. I once actually watched an orchestra so despair of the beat of a conductor, that they resorted to the ancient practice of follow my leader - they turned their attention to the first violin leader, John Fairbairn, and followed him. All the conductor has is a stick. It makes no noise, unless he is desperate enough to rap it on the rail. That is why I will so often use anecdotes about conductors to make points about performance: for a conductor is analogous in his role to a creator God who cannot operate without co-operation. In total contrast to this, the organist is in a position of genuine power, indeed of totalitarian dictatorship. Without effort he can deploy decibels like bombs. It was always an illusion that an American President could wipe out the world by pressing an actual nuclear button, but it is no illusion that an organist can wipe out a congregation by pressing the full organ button. However, fear not, for fear is as poor a guide in matters artistic as spiritual. Like nuclear power, noise cannot be disinvented. Admittedly there is a modern movement in organ building as in orchestral playing of the classics, to return to a baroque scale in instruments, but if an organ is to be able to lead a congregation, then the full organ, even on a baroque instrument, is still going to be a formidable sound. The responsibility of worship is therefore even more keenly laid at the door of the one person controlling that sound - the organist - than at the door of the orchestral conductor, whose responsibility is shared among a large number of instrumentalists.

Who am I to suggest anything more clever here than Sir Adrian Boult did? The organist should aim at an emotional contour for the service. Even if he doesn't know the praise list till he visits the vestry before the service, a very bad practice on the part of clergy, but still a not uncommon one, that still allows a few minutes to assess where the hymnological peaks are likely to be. Perhaps Mount Everest can be descried above distant clouds - a commanding last hymn - and the other climaxes scaled down from that. Possibly there are two Scottish Munros, a strong psalm to begin, an equally strong paraphrase before the sermon, but in this case the emotional peak may be measured not in loudness but in intensity in a devotional hymn in the centre of the service, played quietly with a throbbing pedal to catch the accumulating emotion. The point is not to squander your assets in being either monotonously quiet or monotonously half-loud, and above all not by being monotonously fortissimo. It's a bit like driving a vehicle. If you drive flat out all the time, apart from endangering other road users, and terrorising your own passengers, you are limiting your options, because you have no reserves of power to get out of a sticky situation or exploit an opening. But equally unhelpful is to ramble along at such a monotonous forty miles per hour that you drive other drivers to apoplexy through frustration and fall asleep at the wheel yourself.

That doesn't sound deeply aesthetic or theological. Well, I did say it boiled down to common sense. All I'm saying is, make it interesting. Let go sometimes - be very loud. Be quiet sometimes - very quiet. Take risks. Have variety. But make it a coherent, eloquent variety. Let the whole service say something.

However, there is more than one way to skin a cat, and the Boult way of conducting is not the only one, by a long chalk. I now introduce three remarkable conductors of whose style the very last thing that could be said is that it was monotonous. Each indeed came at different times under the judgement of bad taste, particularly in the matter of speeds. Imaginative flexibility in the speed of hymns is the next weapon I want to identify in the armoury of the anti-monotony effort, so why not learn some lessons from the approach, and the mistakes, of some supreme interpreters?

Paul Kletzki was a Polish conductor, now dead, who had exceptional physical and psychic magnetism. As long ago as 1932, Furtwängler had nominated him to take over the Berlin Philharmonic. But that was ruled out by the Nazis. Kletzki was the Karajan that never was - only, in my opinion, better. He was tall, with a huge forehead, and quite extraordinary eyes. They communicated directly with individual members of the orchestra and the connection often took the form of a brilliant beady wink. The then Scotsman music critic, Christopher Grier, not known as a paid up member of the Mills and Boon School of Criticism, reported that members of what was then the Scottish National Orchestra had fallen in love with Kletzki, and went on to write that he made every instrument sound more individually like itself than was normal. I watched from the Usher Hall organ gallery as Kletzki conducted Brahm's Third Symphony, and was so gripped that I came through to Glasgow the following night to reassure myself that it was as extraordinary as I had thought - and it was. The first movement is difficult to get right in terms of speed. It is a broad six/four sweep, which can't be conducted in six/four beats without sounding fussy, but can, if allowed to broaden too loosely, fail to acquire momentum. Kletzki took it dangerously slowly. It didn't falter, though, far less fall apart, because he implanted within it a deep spring of dynamism. I had the bonus of attending the rehearsal, and heard him rehearse one tiny point - as many would think it - for several minutes. In the eighth bar there is a flourish of two quavers in the tune. I have heard it often under other conductors, and one hardly notices it as an ornamental detail lost in the onward flow. Kletzki took it to bits, trying again and again to coax the violins to treat it as significant, to turn it into a lyrical bridge, a surge of yearning. The same transformation had to occur with the equivalent figure in bar ten.

You may recall what I said earlier about the baaing sheep in the Prague nativity scene - a concept which could have detracted from the overall effect; and I raised the same question with regard to gargoyles and organ screens in cathedrals. Did this lavishing of attention by Kletzki on a detail of phrasing, which amounted to a temporary slowing up of these quavers, impede the onward flow of an already deliberate tempo? It might have. That was a risk. But the effect was the opposite. It converted the surface flow into a profound surge, and this undertow accumulated throughout the symphony, so that when we reached the last movement, its dreamy sunset ending had a hypnotic effect, almost sending orchestra and audience into a trance.

Can I offer an example of such a risk taking in the presentation of a hymn? It is not an exact equivalent, but does illustrate the risk factor in temporarily stretching a tempo. When I first heard W.O.Minay, the organist in St. Cuthberts, Edinburgh (of whom I shall have more to report in Chapter Six), play an Easter service, I was taken aback by his treatment of the second last verse of 'Jesus Christ Is Risen Today'. On the line, "Now above the sky He's King", he applied full reverse thrust on the two words, "He's King" with a strong change of key on "King", and a bold pause, before launching back into tempo. It was spectacular, but risky, because it could have been said to break the back of a climactic verse. A case of you pays your money and you takes your chance. For my money it worked because it rescued the cardinal theological point about the Resurrection from the familiar flow of words and music. It erected, as it were, a musical icon to that central truth which simply couldn't be ignored. I discovered subsequently that that idea originated with Sir Edward Bairstow when organist at York Minster, and it became a tradition at York. So, as always in such cases, an idea which has taken root in different places, began as a risk taken one Easter morning decades ago by one man alone in the organ loft thinking, "I wonder if this will come off", and giving it a whirl. Without that readiness to risk failure and the judgement of bad taste, nothing new will ever be attempted.

My next spectacular conductor is **Leonard Bernstein**. Now Bernstein was something else again: a genius; a cross between Leonardo da Vinci and the Marx Brothers. His 'West Side Story' is a *raison d'être* for the twentieth Century, certainly for that aspect of it known as the United States, but he is capable, in his risk taking of such flights of doubtful taste as to make him *kitsch* king of the symphony. His conducting of Elgar's 'Enigma Variations', transmitted on British television, was electrifying, not merely shaking dust off Elgar's shoes, but hoovering the shoes themselves into an alchemy of the Black Arts. Some of it was refreshing. 'Nimrod', however, was a disaster. I defend to the death Bernstein's courage in going over the top in the matter of tempo, but I defend also my right to assess, as other reviewers did, that in the cause of nobility he obliged too much, bowed too low, sank too deep, and killed the goose that lays the golden egg, namely the tune. He didn't just do it slow. He stopped the clock ticking. He took 'Nimrod' into a time warp. Any slower and it would have gone backwards. There was no pulse at all. The patient had kicked the bucket. How could he? Because he had a mystical vision of something ineffable, beyond the conditions of time. It was a noble mistake, though a mistake it was, for the simple reason that it didn't work.

Sir John Barbirolli did not have to strive to be noble. His was a Napoleonically noble style of arm-waving. In the Royal Festival Hall, in one of his last concerts, he conducted what seemed like a valedictory performance of Elgar's Second Symphony. Time stood still, but in a different sense from Bernstein. Every tempo was elegaically right, and the sunset ending was an apotheosis which sent my wife and me walking along the Thames Embankment in tears.

Nor was the reaction confined to us. From one side of the hall ran Neville Cardus, the celebratory writer on music and cricket; from the other side ran Lord Boothby. In the aisle, they hugged, and their eyes were moist, too. William Mann, the Times critic, wrote the next day that something of an unusually spiritual character had happened during that performance. I discovered much later that Elgar's Second was the music that 'Glorious' John said he would have chosen to die to. I don't know whether he did. I do know that he is the conductor who in my presence most urgently caught the passion in the fugal string passage in the 'Funeral March' in Beethoven's 'Eroica' Symphony. His emphatic forcing of every note built up an almost unbearable tension.

But Barbirolli, too, could nod. Mahler's Ninth Symphony is his valedictory one. The last movement is a subdued howl of a soul facing extinction, transmuted by sobbing stages into a more tranquil but still aching acceptance of diminishment and death which, like Tchaikovsky's Sixth trails into silence. If you compare George Solti's recording with Barbirolli's, Solti's is several minutes shorter. I think sometimes Solti is too crisp. But in this case I find him exactly right. The music sobs enough, it doesn't need amplifying. Barbirolli over-eggs the emotional pudding. It's a great searing performance by the Berlin Philharmonic, but it is too much. The movement, half-way through being milked, capsizes under its own weight. Or so I feel - but *tempi* are always subjective. Are there lessons to be learned from these orchestral experiences which might be applied to hymn-singing?

Take the hymn 'O Love That Wilt Not Let Me Go', a hymn of the deepest subjective hue whose final words we have already quoted. What is to be done with it? Well, I know what is not to be done with it, and that is to dust it down, polish its shoes, smarten up its jacket and tie, slick down its hair, cuff it on the ear, and send it off to 'Songs of Praise' to be toughened up, made to stand straight and turned into a man.

I yield to nobody in my admiration for the classic television formula that 'Songs of Praise' has become, but like all institutions it can sometimes deal insensitively with individual cases. Rows of shiny faces drilled to watch the conductor or die, and deploying dentifugal force as if all singing "cheese" is all very well for Christian soldiers marching onward, but it verges on Gulag treatment for "From the ground there blossoms red, Love that shall endless be". What goes specially wrong is the speed. There has crept into being in recent decades a consensus among many, possibly a majority, of sensible house-trained church musicians that healthy singing doesn't hang about. It's all part of the understandable reaction against lazy sentimentality and loose emotional living down there among the more maudlin Victorian hymnological aspidistras, but it is in danger of becoming a cure as pernicious as the disease. Yes, of course a hymn should not be so slow that, like Bernstein's 'Nimrod', it falls apart in your hands. But, if it is a poem of passionate intensity, set to an appropriately yearning tune, neither should it be set off at a spanking trot to jog four times around the block.

We must have the courage to risk what I have called *kitsch*. Is deep emotion something so dangerous or degrading that we have to throw round it a *cordon sanitaire* of hygienic speeds approved by the local Speed Watch Committee or the Central Board of Time and Motion Studies in the Efficient Management of Praise Resources? Can I take your mind back to the scene in the Prague Church of Holy Mary, Mother of all Angels, when the old priest and the interpreter to President Havel joined in singing about Jesus as the flower from Mary's heart? The

George Matheson words are a kind of Protestant Bultmannian version, are they not, where redemptive love blossoms red not from a Madonna's heart, but from the ground of being.

By a nice piece of serendipity, the next day our little Channel Four Production Unit in Prague attended a morning service of the Czech Evangelical Brethren. It took place in a plain room, and took the form of a hymn sandwich. The young minister spoke and prayed, the congregation of thirty sang. Two of the four Reformation chorales they sang are in our CH3 and were sung crisply, accompanied on the electronic organ with impeccable taste, in the continental reformed style - that is without any deviation whatever of speed or tone colour. This is objective praise, as they see it, and as I was brought for a while to believe in it, when I was a theological student. But it was noticeable that for the children's song, the minister and another young man took guitars and led a song with a swing. I am not guitar-mad, myself, but these were well played, and there is no denying that as they swung slightly and the subjective tune gathered momentum, the quality of the voices was about twice as loud, and, more to the point, twice as warm, as it had been in the hygienically neutral chorales.

Later that day, I was standing in Wenceslas Square in Prague with Bob, our driver, ex-theological student. Beside us was the martyr's grotto. In the centre, a photograph of Jan Palach, the student who immolated himself when Brezhnev's Russian tanks rolled into crush the 1968 Prague Spring. There was a row of photographs of other martyrs of that time. Flowers, candles and coloured ribbons abounded. Artistically, it was a right old mess. Aesthetically, it was *kitsch*. Bob then described the days in November a year before, in which he was intimately involved, when blood ran. Around the grotto, the street was now covered in large, flat paving stones. He said these had been put in to replace the small cobbles which were used to stone the invading tanks. But if one did not know that story, he said wistfully, these would just be dead stones.

Without each human story, hymns are dead stones. Every hymn is a potential nativity, grotto, open wound, open tomb.

Into every hymn, and every performance of every verse of every hymn, should be poured all we can give of our heart's blood, redeemed by as skilled an art as we can manage.

Surrounding this memorial to Palach and the others were curious shapes like twisted mounds of earth. It was a shock to realise that this was the accumulated waste wax of all the candles that had been burned there. Grief, passion, despair, hope, faith, poured together into a mould. When we sing, it may or may not be in good taste, but let it be about something that matters. Music matters because it is about death, and life; it is a mould into which all our deepest discords and harmonies are melted.

On arriving back from Prague, we found on the Euston concourse copies of the Evening Standard with a familiar face on page one. You may have wondered: what have orchestral conductors to do with real life, especially in the modern world? Well, newspaper editors are hard men. They sell newspapers that people want to pick up and read. The photograph was of a conductor. Leonard Bernstein was dead. This composer and performer, whose style of living was as rampantly generous as his style of conducting, had made his last leap into the air. The paper quoted a critic as saying, "Bernstein did not age gently and gracefully. His kind of conducting exacted a high physical toll." To quote the opening paragraph of this chapter, written without knowledge even that Bernstein was ill, "Music is about death. That is why it costs so much. That is why it is worth its weight in gold."

The article went on to say, "Bernstein's performances were subject to human error, but they came into the world bloody and pink and blue, kicking and screaming, laughing and crying." That isn't a bad motto for those responsible, in towns and villages up and down our land, for the musical aspect of our worship. If our music, and especially our singing, seems sometimes becalmed, if not dead in the water, perhaps that is because we are more concerned to avoid error than to kickstart worship into life. What about a policy of bringing, for example, hymns into a Sunday morning, "bloody and pink and blue, kicking and screaming, laughing and crying."

Music is about death. Music confronts death. Music defeats death. Mendelssohn and Brahms are biologically dead. But an orchestra they conducted played recently in Glasgow: the Leipzig Gewandhaus Orchestra in its Brahms season played not only the Third Symphony, but all four. The conductor was Kurt Mazur. What was my question: what have conductors to do with the modern world? It was the wordsmith Havel who carried the day for freedom in Prague. In East Germany, it was a conductor, Mazur himself, who at a couple of critical moments used his influence with both the old government and the crowd to enable a public debate to take place. Mazur had no party power. But, to allow free communication to flow, for the sake of the possibility of a rebirth of his people and culture, he risked arrest and death. If the Christian idea of Resurrection means anything, it means that whatever is about Death is about Birth also. Whatever is about human error is also about divine freedom. So on the Glasgow train we acquired champagne in the buffet car, and toasted Bernstein as a human being who will never be dead, for the tunes and discords of his life have melted into moments of glory on wax, that we can hear every time a disc or tape reveals again his brave risks with taste. For glory is not about being always right. It is about being.

Chapter Three

SILENCE IS GOLDEN

You won't have too much difficulty, perhaps, in bringing to mind that moment when on a muggy summer's evening you put some blocks of ice into a glass. Clunk... clunk. You unscrew the white cap of the green bottle, and pour... glug, glug. Hissssssss. The glass mists over as the gin hits the ice. Unscrew the tonic. Pour it. Sshusshhh, and you-know-who bubbles. Slice a lemon, squeeze its droplets out, let it go... splash. Another gentle hiss.

Now comes the moment you've been waiting for. Lift the glass to your mouth, sip, and let a chilled rivulet trickle over the teeth and down the gullet. There it flows - that sensation of coolness tingling its way to near and distant parts.

That is a function of religious music. And unless you are running a cathedral, it is cheaper than gin. Also, music doesn't attack your brain cells, your stomach, your liver. It may, like gin, go for your larynx if you are a participator, but this is not usually lethal. On the other hand, like gin and tonic, or whatever your favourite summer tipple is - white wine, cider, beer, apple juice, orange juice, milk shake, chilled coffee - a vital function of church music is to release you from the sweaty grip of moral perspiration into a cooler, spaced-out world of inspiration; where, as the Latin word *spiro* implies, you can breathe more easily and deeply, stand back from life's tactical skirmishes - even from its moral and religious tactical skirmishes - interpret your situation as a whole, or, to paraphrase Wordsworth, re-assemble hot-house emotional furniture in tranquility. This is at least one function of art, and music can be the purest art, though I concede that religious music does not always attain that level.

For those who are alienated by an alcoholic reference, or who feel that a cold October night is not the time to be lyrical about summer drinking, I postulate, not a July day, but a February one, majoring in slush, depression, and the kind of chill in your bones which makes global warming beckon like a free weekend in the Caribbean. You stumble in the front door, kick the frozen slush off your wellies, trip over the dog doing his ham imitation of an underfed Husky, turn on the kettle, throw the day's booty of milk, bread and catfood into the pile of unwashed dishes, put a teabag in a mug, pour in the boiling water, add milk, prise with a frozen finger a digestive biscuit out of a blue tin, grimace at the yellow daffodils on the blue tin, heave your carcass on to a stool, lift the mug to your lips and... aaaah... hot tannin carries adrenalising caffeine to every corner of your besieged cadaver.

This also, in the icy wastes of a myth-frozen culture, is a prime function of music, church or otherwise - to thaw out the parts that you thought would never feel anything ever again - to restore the circulation of the heart's blood.

These are two functions of church music, to cool and to warm. But there is another. After all, we do not spend most of our existence ambushed by extremes of hot and cold. We live in a temperate zone. Our religion is not characteristically overheated by emotion or spectacularly frozen by intellect. Just as, compared with other parts of the world, our summers are relatively cool, and our winters relatively mild, so our religion is relatively undramatic, neither very up or very down, pretty straightforward middle of the road stuff. Yet we sing in church. Why? Well, there is a third kind of liquid we imbibe. Water. In one form or another, water is built into our diet. Sometimes, these days, as when one grills factory processed bacon, water seems built excessively into our food. As you know, most of the human body is composed of water. Without water, we die. I am so bold as to suggest that the reason even we undemonstrative Northern Europeans do this irrational thing in church of opening the hole in our face and throwing our voice up and down a bit without any obvious practical motive - is that, if we don't, our religion dies.

How can I say that, when one Christian group greatly respected for its uncluttered spirituality positively glories in not doing this thing? The Society of Friends makes a point of silence, does it not? Ah, well. In the first place, Quakers are much less bureaucratic about such things than we think. They are human, sensitive beings, who love to listen to music, and can sing as well as anyone. But, in the second place, what is silence? The absence of sound? I doubt if you have ever heard the absence of sound? How could you hear it, if it is not there? You cannot prove a negative. Put it this way: have you ever experienced the absolute absence of liquid? No - if liquid was entirely absent, you'd be dead. If sound was entirely absent, you'd be - no, not deaf, even stone deaf people have mental sensations corresponding to sound - but again, dead. When the composer John Cage, in his composition 4'33", instructed the pianist to sit for four and a half minutes and do nothing, he was not inviting the audience into an experience where sound was absent. On the contrary, he was luring us into a recognition of the music in the sounds that are everywhere around us. BBC engineers do not allow the absence of sound, although for a very special effect they may come near it with white noise - a sort of acoustic equivalent of a Black Hole, sucking into its mystical negativity any light energy foolish enough to stray within a few zillion miles. Transmitters shut down if there is not some texture of noise, even if the casual listener, hearing on an average domestic receiver, might interpret it as silence. But that is an interpretation. Silence is not a physical reality: it is a metaphysical, an abstract concept.

If we can take this one way and say that silence is actually quite noisy, we can take it the other way and say that noise can be - in the metaphysical sense that is its only real sense - quite silent. I recall several moments in my life when, in purely decibelic terms an acoustic experience was such that I must filch from the great preacher J.S. Stewart one of his most decisive adjectival exocets - SHATTERING - the noise was shattering, yet the effect on my brain was to create internally an awesome silence. I recall a couple of such occasions in the Usher Hall, at early Edinburgh Festivals. Ian Hunter, the Scots impresario who brilliantly laid the foundations of the Festival, brought over the orchestra and chorus of La Scala, Milan, and they sang Verdi's Requiem, twice. I was there, twice. On the second occasion, the tumult in the hall caused such a tumult in my psychic system that I spent an entire night on Blackford Hill encountering a brilliant God who didn't so much demand my life as simply occupy it - to such an extent that when I arrived home for breakfast my mother said, "This is what comes of not having enough fresh air and vegetables."

But that was after the second performance. Two nights before I had heard Verdi's Requiem for the first time. Heard? What does "heard" mean? This is not a silly question. That figure who strolls, strides, lounges, lunges, and finally self-destructs his way through the Gospel narratives certainly had sufficient reservations about the listening function to lob a couple of paradoxes in its direction. The disciples were exasperated literally beyond belief, perhaps, by the cryptic epigrams, stories, and filmic sequences which Jesus transmitted instead of clear moral service announcements, or pharisaic party political hard sells, but when they yelped, "Why do you make it so difficult, why do you tell things in parables?" Jesus' answer is a model side-swerve: "I tell things in parables so that people may hear and not understand." One might rephrase that apparently less than helpful remark, something like this:

> I tell it in parables so that the message may mean something special to those who not only take in the words as an acoustic phenomenon activating the eardrum, but receive the metaphysical light contained within the sound package. Then the light may burst open within the inner ear and spread radiance into the farthest recesses of that auditorium which is the human brain, that cathedral which is the human personality, that ultimate human reality which no theologian or acoustic scientist can measure.

That is true hearing, that is real listening. And the effect can be a devastating inner silence: because, faced with the blinding light of an ultimate truth, there is nothing left to say. Jesus' other repeated advice was: "He who hath ears, let him hear." I needn't labour that point. Clearly, the possession of two pieces of radar equipment sticking at right angles to the head does not, in Jesus' assessment, necessarily constitute what He thinks of as hearing.

Well, there I was forty years ago, in the 'gods' of the Usher Hall, about to 'hear' Verdi's Requiem for the first time. The organ gallery was pulsating with Mediterranean vibrations - the La Scala Chorus, a couple of hundred Latin temperaments shimmering like the original cosmic material awaiting its Big Bang. Victor de Sabata, the conductor, loped on from the wings, a sinister amalgam of Boris Karloff and Batman. During the Requiem, as much of his time was spent off the rostrum as on it, his vertical take-offs suggesting attempts by an alien octopoid to extract electrical voltage from high wire pylons above the Usher Hall roof. Nothing, however, prepared one for the assault of the 'Dies Irae', the wrath of God. As it began, extra brass pullulated in doors on both sides of the hall. They were breeding like cockroaches. Everywhere, trumpets were rampaging, and trombones marching like Birnam Wood on Dunsinane. I see yet de Sabata shaking demonic fists and damning us all to Hell, as, flying through the air, he detonated the Apocalypse. The din was appalling. And what I experienced was: absolute silence. It was a moment of reality. Time stopped. Watches ceased ticking. The door of the eternal opened. That, if you please, is silence, and a Quaker need have no quarrel with that. Nor need an agnostic, an atheist, a Buddhist, a Hindu, any human soul. This kind of metaphysical silence I equate with another condition, perhaps best described as seriousness. One might even say: high seriousness.

Let me try and explain that by referring to another Festival occasion in the Usher Hall: a performance of Bach's B Minor Mass by the Huddersfield Choral Society and the Liverpool Philharmonic, conducted by Malcolm Sargent. I had only experienced this work (WORK? - this cantilever bridge across eternity) once before, when my music teacher at Fettes, Tommy Evans, had taken a group of us to a performance by the then Edinburgh Royal Choral Union under Herrick Bunney, in St. Giles Cathedral. On the way, Tommy Evans said, "This is possibly the greatest single piece of music ever written", so our expectations were not slim as we climbed the Mound to St. Giles. Herrick told me, years later, that it had been a disastrous performance, because he was new, both to the choir and St. Giles, and hadn't realised how manifold and deadly were the acoustic ambushes laid by the reverberations in the St. Giles nooks and crannies; so there were moments when basses in one far-flung contrapuntal galaxy were in telepathic rather than metronomic communication with tenors spiralling up the outermost arm of distant fugal nebulae. Herrick was obviously a better judge of the details of the choral ensemble than I, so if he says there were problems, then there were problems, but what I heard exalted me. In the Sanctus the angels swung their censers and the earth moved. The basses and organ pedal growled around the perimeter of space as the 'Et Incarnatus' and 'Crucifixus' sank through the transdimensional trapdoor. If that was my first experience of the 'B Minor', what was to happen when Sargent, the most brilliant choral conductor of his age, brought his favourite well drilled choir to bear on the masterpiece? Again: silence. As the final chord of 'Dona Nobis Pacem' ended, my thought was: "I can never laugh again." That was pompous, fey, callow; but it was so intensely felt that I can recall the exact sensation. If any human being can be this serious, I said to myself, if life is worth this degree of seriousness, then I am silent before life. I cannot pollute the silence with words; and never again am I free to laugh.

Well, one's late teens are a time for such gargantuan solemnity. But I wouldn't devalue that response, not even now that I am on my way to garrulous geriatricity. It had been a transfiguring experience. So it was with eagerness that I subsequently opened my Scotsman to read the review of the performance. It was of the "this hurts me more that it hurts you" variety. The then Scotsman music critic, Stewart Deas, was not lukewarmly on the fence. Let your yea be yea, and your nay be nay. His nay was nay, alright. He excoriated Sargent for turning in a sub-Festival performance where the Horn had fluffed a note or two in its solo obligato in the 'Quoniam'; but even more heavily he laid into Sargent for putting too much dramatic emphasis on the final chord of each chorus. I'm not saying

Stewart Deas was making technically invalid points, just that, in terms of our inner hearing, he and I might have been in different halls hearing different performances.

That is why public reviews of performances should, in my view, always include a celebratory element, so that, whatever happens, you wish you had been there, if you weren't, and you're glad you were, if you were: rather than looking embarrassedly over your shoulder and thinking: "Oh, I missed that technical point, so it wasn't so good", as if your experience was less authentic than the reviewer's. As it happens the present policy of Glasgow Herald reviewing is under Michael Tumelty tumultuously of the celebratory kind - indeed it may swing the other way so that you think: "My goodness, if it was that mind-blowing, why didn't my mind blow?" Well, that's a fault in the right direction, an excess of enthusiasm is still a breathing of the spirit. But even though the Scotsman's ex-critic Conrad Wilson, like Christopher Grier before him, could be waspish in the best Eastern Wasp manner, there was style and eloquence in reserve to give emotional body to his technical assessments. His successor, Mary Miller, writes like an angel, yet, like Wilma Paterson at the Herald, without sacrificing tough musical criteria. All this matters, because you have to decide whether evaluating music, analysing it, writing about it, is a branch of showbusiness or of academia.

I will have more to say of this later, because it goes back to the question of what is being heard, who is doing the hearing, and what the whole performing and hearing process is in aid of. It is in aid of people. Music is not in the first place a matter of abstract principle, but of experience, and I do not know of any currency other than experience the truth of whose coinage can better stand the test of time. After all, if experiences are vivid after forty years they must have amounted to something. On the other hand, I realise that if I am to continue to wander up paths of reminiscence, then you are entitled to be reminded of the general direction in which we are heading: which is that as much as liquid is essential for life, so as vital for religious life is music. But that immediately led to a consideration of traditions of spirituality which are less vocal, and we have been thinking

about what spiritual or emotional silence is: our tentative
conclusion being that it does not depend on the absence of
music, still less on the absence of sound. That is where we are,
and I would like to stay there a little longer.

Think of the wasp. Not the waspish critic, but the common or
garden black and yellow buzzing wasp. Can you, in your
mind's ear, hear it? Now consider the bumble bee. This also is
black and yellow. Possibly the yellow verges on the orange. The
clothing is furrier. The general effect is less sleek and missile-
like. But compared with the elephant, whale, or even bluebottle, markedly the same. Now hear the bee buzz. In your
auditory opinion, are these buzzes markedly different? I mean,
put you in an airtight sound studio, place earphones on your
head, and play in tapes of wasp and bee in an unknown order,
are you confident you could say which was which?

But now we'll change the scenario. We'll blindfold you and
lead you into a garden. It is June. Your nose is wafting in
perfume of box, lavender, roses. The sun beats. Birds twitter.
There is buzzing. You don't have to ask. It is bees, it is beautiful,
it is eternal childhood summer. God's in His heaven and all is
lazily right in a bee-loud world.

But be led now, if you please, to a small stuffy room in
August. There is tea on the table. Raspberry jam sits around,
awaiting union with a scone. Your companion gives an exasperated squawk. A newspaper goes thwack on the table. Irritation
is in the air. Something is buzzing. Guess what? No prizes for
guessing: a wasp.

Don't tell me your ear told you the difference. It was the
whole picture, the general environment, and - more - the myth
attached to the situation that led you to hear one thing rather
than another. It was a composite constellation of images in your
brain, an imaginative package, which said bee or wasp.

In that sense, the actual notes, or even the sequence of notes,
in a piece of music is not the message. Without the notes, a piece
of music doesn't exist, as without the buzz, no bee, no wasp. But
the notes in themselves don't tell you what is going on. Your
imagination does. Therefore, worry not if your church lacks

organ, choir, or brilliant musician. We all have imaginations.
That is the chief resource of church music, and it is free. If there
is any one reason why these days music is not the thrilling
element in church worship that it might be, it is that we all let
our imaginations lie moribund. Twelve people in a congregation, released from inhibition as they are seized by the vast
import of the words of a hymn or psalm, can lift not only the
indifferent singing of a scattered congregation, but also the
indifferent playing of an organ presided over by a poor player.

I'm not saying that the performance at the organ doesn't
matter. Imagination there can lift everybody. Obviously, there
is interpretation of music in all performances. We will of course
return to that topic frequently - for the music doesn't exist
unless the notes are lifted off the page by a human being or
beings who by an alchemy nobody really understands recreate
an emotional earthquake experienced by a brain which for 200
years may have lain decomposed beneath the ground. But have
you considered the mirror miracle: how did those notes arrive
on the page in the first place? Some composers composed at the
piano, but more heard the music in their head. How did that
happen? The ear was not involved. There was no sound at all.
And they weren't hearing through memory, because the music
was, as of that moment, being created *ex nihilo*. 'The Messiah',
the 'Mass in B Minor', Mozart's 'Eine Kleine Nachtmusik',
Beethoven's 9th, Tchaikovsky's 5th, Wagner's Ring, 'Abide
with Me'. These were heard before they were heard: How?
Heard in absolute silence! Not bad little on-board computers
the great composers had, in those pre-computer days. The
Jehovah of Israel and the Father of our Lord Jesus Christ was,
for a pre-Luddite, not a bad knocker together of information
technology systems.

You will by now perceive what I'm getting at. I'm trying to
demythologise music - or is it re-mythologise it? I'm saying
there isn't a thing which you can identify as music. Music is
wider than any definition you can give it. Music is, in fact, a
way. A way of being, a way of loving, a way of worshipping, a
way of understanding. A way of sympathising, empathising,
synthesising. Music is a way of being born, or being re-born, of

being crucified, resurrected, transformed. Music is a way of life. Music is a way of dancing on the edge of thinking. And, above all, music is a way of listening. Only at the end, and at the margins, and at the bottom of that list, is music a technique of organising sounds.

Certain conclusions follow. Music in the church is far too important to be left to church musicians. But equally, music is far too important to be left to the priest at the altar, or the minister in the pulpit. It is too important even to be left to the theologian or liturgical expert laying down what worship is about. And, equally, music is far too important to be left to one person seated at the organ, or the enthusiastic choir-master, or the soprano who always gets the solos. Or the junior choir who have to be encouraged. And, finally, music is too precious to be left to the loudest voices 'in the pew' who know what they like, want what they like, and will make everyone else uncomfortable till they get it. All these, of course, have a role to play. The role of some will be functionally, if not spiritually, more central than the role of others, but the interplay, and proportion of these roles will vary from one place to another - will vary, indeed, to such a gigantic extent that it is virtually fruitless, certainly very difficult, to suggest general rules for the conduct of music in church. One fundamental point I hope to make in these lectures is that nothing kills the potential of music more stone dead than a conventional assumption as to who does what and how. Because if music is a general way of approaching reality, of dealing with life, of living, then there are as many approaches to music, and experiences of music, as there are sentient beings.

That is even more true if there is any validity to the even wider point I'm making, which is that music is not in essence to do with sound patterns, but with an apprehension of life which I will be content for the moment to label as lateral, intuitive, irrational. That is not to say it ignores the rational, the formal, the linear, the argumentative, the intellectual. Who could say that intellect was absent from a fugue of Bach, the sonata form of a Haydn symphony, the epic developments of a Beethoven symphony, the steel and silk counterpoint of a

Shostakovich symphony; but who could doubt that what is lacking in the equally clever mathematical computation of the brilliant music student who never becomes a great composer is an extra dimension and that extra dimension is of the essence: and that extra dimension can be in the simplest hymn tune or popular ballad. Looked at mathematically, a great song of Cole Porter, Irving Berlin or Lloyd Webber is probably not intricate enough to be academically interesting, though if you do analyse it it will possibly bear examination even on those terms. But what is the genius of it? And why is 'Still The Night' a great carol? Clive James has a nice phrase in one of his classic TV reviews in the Observer in the Seventies. He observes that humour is common sense, dancing. Let us say that music is: thinking, dancing. I say thinking advisedly, because if music is feeling only, it does degenerate; and you've only to switch on Radio Two or listen to certain evangelical or charismatic songs to know where that takes you.

Music, then, is not an objective pattern of sound waves available for hearing. It is what you hear. But also, music is not just what you hear. It is an amalgam of what you hear and the way you hear it. But even the what you hear element is wider than what we commonly call music.

Nowhere is this mutual interdependence of music and environment more obvious than in a great cathedral. You wander in on a dark afternoon in November. There is no choir, no service in progress, not even a choir rehearsal. A few tourists move slowly up the aisles in and out of shadows, sit in side chapels. Shafts of pale winter sunlight abseil down the nave from windows high in the tower. You sit in wonderment. Your spirit opens up to the unity in complexity of all that you see. More than that, your brain responds to the intellectual power of the environment. The massive forces matching gravity, exploiting it, playing with it, turn stone into counterpoint; the vast mythology is compressed into medieval glass, even though, being no longer medieval, you do not have the time to absorb it; subliminally it triggers your brain's capacity to recognise magical order. The whole experience is already a symphony, a tone-poem, a master fugue. Yet the organ hasn't sounded one note. The only sounds are those arbitrary little bangs, thuds, and squeaks never absent from a huge living building. Then, quite unexpectedly, out of the blue, out of the shadows, out of the eternal *nihilo*, sounds a profound organ pedal note. It is quiet, a sixteen foot Bourdon perhaps, but it stirs something within you.

That note is pregnant with yet unborn implications. Although it is only one note, and so low that you can hardly identify it as a note in a scale, let alone a key which might contextualise it, in other words although it can hardly yet be said to be music, its vibrations steal over the vast shadowy structure, beginning to ebb and flow like waves. Well of course, they are sound waves - encroaching on every gap and space in the cathedral and within the network of your receptive senses. All this is but the work of seconds, yet in that time timeless apertures are opened. But what is it going to be? Bach, Caesar Franck, Herbert Howells? Like a flower opening to the sun, your inner ear has been triggered by a thousand messages connecting the tendrils of your spirit to the musical mouth of the eternal which a cathedral plus one organ note is. For just as music is not a sequence of notes, so an organ is not a collection of pipes. An organ is the instrument called the organ plus the instrument which is its echoing chamber, in this case the cathedral. But you are still waiting to hear what specific musical world is to unfold from that first penumbral stirring. A second note follows, a semitone up. Then a third, another semitone. This is going to be a chromatic adventure - Franck or Howells, somehow it feels too deliberately paced for Messiaen. But now, the fugitive harmonics are merging in the cathedral's resonance. The building is being slowly massaged into a soft perturbation. More notes follow. It is a chromatic scale.

By the time you have realised what is going on, namely that the organ tuner has come back after his pie and pint at the pub to continue his day's organ tuning work, it is too late to deconstruct your emotional response. Upon a few unmusical acoustic signals your imagination has created an edifice of expectation. You heard, in anticipation, musical landscapes opening out in the brains of Bach, Franck, and Howells. They never actually took place, but for a while they might as well have, for, like the bee in the garden, the buzzing of this sixteen foot pipe was amplified and coloured in your brain by the whole environment. So in a timeless moment your whole being was responsive to a myth. It wasn't a con. A myth is not a trick, not an illusion. A myth is the world you live in, using all the materials that are available. In that sense music is myth and church music is liturgical myth. What is required to make the mythical potential come alive is not brilliance, but a willingness by average people to engage in risky alchemy.

Let me offer an example from the world of films, an appropriate enough medium for comparison, for you could argue that in the 20th Century film is the common liturgy. Television might seem a competitive candidate for such a title, but the specific requirements which liturgy imposes - coming together at a given time and place - are missing in television, quite apart from the atmospheric components of hush, dimmed lights, a cultic jargon, and a sense of expectation.

What does Australia say to you? 'Neighbours', of course. One has to time the switching on of the BBC 6 o'clock news to the second to avoid the last bars of the 'Neighbours' jingle which sticks to the aural palate like a cupful of saccharine. Australia also means Clive James and Dame Edna Everage, and the older ones amongst us recall other references. There is an old fashioned Australian tune called 'Waltzing Matilda'. It is an unofficial Australian National Anthem like 'Scots Wha Hae' or 'Auld Lang Syne'. It jogs along quite nicely.

In the 1950s I went with some fellow theological students to the Cameo Cinema in Edinburgh to see the film, 'On The Beach', based on the Neville Shute novel of that title. Apart from the psychologically intriguing fact that a couple of the students who were American walked out in protest at what they took to be an implied criticism of U.S.A. strategic nuclear policy, what remains with me after nearly forty years is one film sequence. The basic scenario is that there has been a devastating nuclear exchange in the Northern Hemisphere, from which all communication has ceased. The film takes place mainly in Australia, where people become gradually aware that the radioactive fall-out will eventually reach them. An American submarine happens to be in Australian waters and eventually sets out northwards to San Francisco to discover what if any life is left. A wide aerial shot of the sub shows it as a frail little craft voyaging on a vast ocean, seeming to carry on its back not only the hopes and fears of the Southern Hemisphere but vicariously the sins of the human species. Is this the Apocalypse, or is there another chance? Ulysses setting out across the Ionian Sea did not carry such a burden. Is there a light, a life, a future, beyond the horizon? Is there a wife to return to, a city, a civilisation, anything?

I thought it a genuinely epic moment, that one wide shot of a little grey sub alone on a southern sea, and in that old film of the 50s it pressed on one's spirit with the urgency of an ominous reality. A true myth took shape in front of one's eyes. Now what music would you match to that? Siegfried's journey down the Rhine? The closing pages of 'Götterdämmerung'? Mahler's 'Song of the Earth'? Or a commissioned score from Tippett?

What we got was 'Waltzing Matilda'.

Ah, you laughed. You were meant to. But listen. Whoever wrote the score had woven 'Waltzing Matilda' as a leitmotif through the film, adapting it to different moods. That sort of thing can be wearisome. But at this moment the score pulled off an emotional coup. Pillars of brass emerging from surging seas of strings alchemised the tune into a massive adagio statement. Heard by itself it might have seemed pastiche Elgar or just genuine Hollywood; but then, you see, genuine Hollywood, as well as British film studios, can be impressive both in craftsmanship and emotional integrity. The import of the passage lay in its association with the immense implications of the story and its visual frame at that moment. Musically, the strength of the passage lay in the crunch discord at its emotional heart, resolved by heroic octaves in the bass.

You will expect me to say what I am going to say, so I will say it. It was hymn-like. And there is no reason why even quite modest organists cannot attempt to lift out of the treasure chest of our hymn books moments of like splendour. A hymn story not so epic? The Bible is a library of just such Odysseys. The absence of film images? The preacher's task is to create them. But also many churches convey a sense of bigness and space; and the words of the hymns frequently carry resonant images. The music not always inspired? The hymnary contains hundred of tunes as good as or far better than 'Waltzing Matilda'. The urgency missing? In an average congregation there is more real-life drama, encompassing vast sadnesses, terrors, and joys, than 'Neighbours' will have in a year. The lack of ability of the organist? It doesn't take brilliance - just a willingness to take emotional risks.

If there is one fundamental message I would like to convey in these modest exercises of reflection, it is this: that each person and group is responsible for creating and living appropriate and possible myths, with whatever materials are available.

In the case of the Baird lectures, for example, I realised I had better practise what I'm preaching. The original idea was to make them thoroughly audio-visual. Having spent most of my working life in broadcasting, with all the riches of radio and video and film available, it was tempting to enrich lectures on church music by washing the eye with images and feeding the ear with all the finest organs, orchestras, choirs, massed congregations in Europe. But gradually, as I considered what all this was about, these ideas retreated down the shingle of the audio-visual world. In the end, it became a question of integrity and trust. Integrity in the sense of trusting one's materials. I was asked to give lectures. And I was given a beautiful hall in which to deliver words. Was it an environment for technical props? For an electronic organ? A piano was in residence, and that fitted the ambience of the exquisite room. But more than that, I considered that the average minister, organist, choir-leader, Sunday-school teacher, worshipper, starts with not more than this: a room, hall, auditorium, church. One instrument. An hour to fill. It would, I concluded, be gross cynicism to bring people into that place, fill their ears with lush sounds brought effortlessly from other times and places and distract their eyes with images of huge crowds brought together in, say, 'Songs of Praise', in circumstances totally abnormal for the normal congregation, and then after that send people back to what they would consider to be reality.

And then I came to the kernel of the matter, that music is something wider than rows of notes. It is an approach to life, a way of conducting one's mind, and, therefore also, a way of using words. Which means, in passing, that the clergy's proper contribution is not to tell the organist or choirmaster how to do their job, but to use pulpit and altar professionalism to approach words in the spirit of that ultimate word, the logos, which I guess is more like music than anything else. As my thoughts unravel, we will open up the musical box in various ways; for the main part, however, words are the materials I must use.

Let me, then in this continuing word exploration of the width of the concept of music, lift the curtain on some contrasting liturgical events. Ah, you think, is he actually going to get near the subject of church music at last? No, probably not, at least not in the sense of addressing practical problems in a systematic way. What I am still trying to do is to show how music in and out of the liturgy interconnects, for the basic reason that life itself is liturgy. For those who, as Jesus said, have ears to hear, the rhythms of daily life contain within them the springs of eternal action.

First I take you to the parish of Ardersier, half way between Nairn and Inverness. I can't take you into the actual church where my uncle exercised for almost half a century his single and singular ministry; for a few years back, the church, originally in the centre of the rural parish, was made redundant. No longer, now, do villagers walk the two miles to join small farmers scattered around in the parish graveyard before being summoned in by the bell. So the church building was demolished. But I could take you to that still used graveyard and tell you of an Easter Sunday morning when my uncle opened up to me the central mystery of Christianity and the single most beguiling secret of the Gospels: the strangely close presence of the other.

The music that Sunday morning fell short of Sydney Smith's celestial prescription: eating *paté de foie gras* to the sound of trumpets. The organ was no organ, if contingent on the *bene esse* of organ-ness is the possession of pipes. It was what my old friend and teacher Bill Minay called a hargroanium. It had transatlantic pretensions, burdened as it was with the title American organ. Which side, one wondered, was it on in the American Civil War? Did Scarlett O'Hara, singing Dixie, the sunset in her hair, ride it at the head of a weary Confederate rabble; or did this noble piece of brown furniture lead posses of Yankee troops to 'Mine Eyes Have Seen The Glory Of The Coming Of The Lord?' Certainly the instrument was battle weary. A handy tube of glue was a *sine qua non*, as in fluctuating temperatures the sharps and flats fell on to the floor like autumn leaves. To this Cinderella, my uncle played prince. After announcing the psalm or hymn, he processed down the pulpit steps and with his ramrod back and shock of white hair sat at the organ, pumped the footbellows, and led us in praise. Unlike President Ford, he could do two things at once, pump and play, but not three. The counting of verses had to be the work of another, to wit my aunt. Her task was to remove her spectacles at the beginning of the last verse. Occasional *lacunae* in this department led my uncle to extend hymns beyond the inspiration of the original author, and the congregation to become adept at inventing lyrics to cover these *ex gratia* verses.

You can picture the scene, then. Elements of bathos, inadequacy, even farce. A long way from the glories of Easter Sunday in Durham Cathedral, which I have three times experienced, or in Canterbury Cathedral, experienced once. Yet... this Ardersier Easter has pervaded my life for longer than these. You see, I have not yet told you all about the music. I haven't told you about the early summer bluebottle or bee drowsily buzzing on the window ledge during the prayers. I haven't mentioned the chirrupings and chortlings of early arrivals on the courting, mating, and nesting front. Or the tantalising drone of Lysanders and Beauforts circling Inverness Airport, then, during the war, a training aerodrome. Or the grass growing outside. Or the painful, tender vulnerability of cracked old country voices mingling with treble pipings from apple-cheeked children. But I've meanly kept the best till last. The organ itself. Yes, no pipes. Yes, in poor repair. Yes, played by an eccentric clergyman, who, though a wondrous pastor was on the organ stool no John Langdon, Walter Blair, or George McPhee. Ah, but... this machine spoke so sweetly. Those who built it were craftsmen of their kind. Its pulchritudinous shimmerings conjured up lutes and flutes heard in a Sylvan scene. Or, at a pinch, it could have been the strings and flutes of a French cathedral organ floating out across a high Gothic transept at evening.

How can this be? Well, years later I had the curious experience of playing a harmonium under the direction of Sir Thomas Beecham. It was a performance of 'L'Enfance du Christ' by Berlioz. A choir of angels sang off-stage, to the side of the Usher Hall organ gallery - outside that very door through which the La Scala squadrons of brass had unleashed Verdi's hounds of hell. This time the sound was very different - the angels of Heaven, tender, sweet, and reassuring. For this the Berlioz score required, not any old harmonium, but a particular make which, in the event, had to be brought across from Paris just for this one performance under my reverential fingers. I'm not saying that the old Ardersier instrument was of that calibre of refinement, but I am pointing out that we categorise at our peril. Pipes good, everything else bad, will not serve in the real world, even the real world of art. My music professor Sidney Newman once said to us music students: "You'll spend 90% of your time moving music stands." This he meant as a parable. Begin with what you have. Dream, yes, but work your dreams through your basic material.

This then, was the musical background for the treasure that my uncle was to reveal. And what was this? I tread softly here, for I tread on the dreams of decades of summers, winters, Christmasses and Easters, shimmering cadences of emotional cloud wisping across the sky of one's life till they merge at the edge of one's imaginative horizon with those first intimations of immortality of which one hesitates to speak lest they crumble in the mouth.

But, simply, my uncle opened the Bible and talked. He read the story of the meeting on the Emmaus Road. He spoke of friendship. He said that the other, the friend we need, is always there, with us, in the presence of others, or alone, invisibly. It was as simple as that. The universe is not an enemy, but a friend. It was as simple as the music we had sung, as transparent as the windows through which I saw the clouds bundle along and the birds cavort. It was as artless as the highest art. So it has stayed with me for ever. Do not, therefore, tell me that a renewal of the magic of church music requires enormous resources, any more than you can persuade me that a renewed mission in Scotland requires either Billy Graham or a new "strategy for outreach".

But next, I take you to St. Giles Cathedral. The contrast could not be more bizarre. Easter Sunday in St. Giles was a packed house, with (in the fifties) a still healthy organ in full cry. Happiness was a Herrick high on horn-piping Handel and a Harry hilariously hoisting hymns into hypostasis. Harry was Harry Whitley, the new minister, and thereby hangs this tale. The tradition in St. Giles had been that at the conclusion of that part of the Great Communion Service which precedes the carrying in of the elements, that part of the congregation which did not intend to partake of communion was invited to leave; at which point a substantial quantity of bums separated from seats, some belonging to tourists, some to conscientious abstainers, some just to those more inclined to wrap their tongue around a sparkling G. & T., or a sherry with more bite than a quaff of dull and serious communion wine. Harry Whitley did not only recognise the liturgical tawdriness of all this, but he felt deep down in his bones - and he was not one to disobey his bones - that at Easter this bucking of the climactic liturgical act of the Christian year, this breaking of its rhythmic spine, was an act of sacrilege, an act ultimately of unreality. I don't think it is going too far to say that he felt that to kill stone dead a liturgical movement that sweeps by inexorable logic of theology, word, poetry and choreography towards its crisis in the re-breaking of bread and re-spilling of wine, and thus through divine catharsis to redemptive hope and resurrected living - to kill that for reasons of convenience was to re-crucify Christ. So he announced his intention to carry the service through from beginning to end without a break. Many in the Kirk Session were aghast. The Senior Minister, Charles Warr, shook his head. Chickens, it was implied, were coming home to roost. Even Whitley supporters went slightly green at the gills. It will be chaos, was the general advice. But for Harry more was at stake than human order, even liturgical human order.

I was in the organ loft that extraordinary Easter morning, and heard and saw it all. The atmosphere was electric. At eleven, the choir processed and Herrick, taking the organ by the scruff of its then considerable neck, heaved it into the front line of the Apocalypse, all guns blazing, the sky lit up by tracering mixtures, St. Giles' old pillars pulverised by pedal panegyrics. Lifted straight out of this gorgeous organistic mayhem like the morning star itself released from the craw of creation, the Whitley voice flashed skyward in a cry of joy indistinguishable from pain. "The Lord is risen. The Lord is risen indeed."

I seldom, if ever, heard a declamation of such primeval force. All in Harry Whitley's journey of faith that he was on this day staking on an act of liturgical recklessness went into that moment of cosmic exposure: for when any human spirit stakes all, it is the cosmic in all its divine brilliance that is exposed. And that is music indeed.

The service, lifted by that rare pair of liturgical twins, the organist Bunney and minister Whitley, climbed through one ecstatic moment after another. Then came the place for the usual break. But this time no announcement about leaving. No invitation for those who wished communion to come up into the choir and make a nice orderly congregation, and the rest to go home for lunch. Just no commercial break at all. The Elders processed out and back in with the elements. Doubt and confusion arose. So did people. As Harry proceeded with the Great Statements and Prayers, more and more sightseers, trapped into a commitment they did not wish to make, began like late theatregoers to push past knees and make for the exits. The lonely voice was at times drowned out by a bustle like Glasgow Airport on a Bank Holiday.

I will draw a veil over the confusion. The post-mortem was painful. I can only declare how I saw it then. For me it was one of the sublime liturgical experiences of my life. I have heard the

Communion Service read hundreds of times, and have read it myself more than a few. I've heard it read quietly, loudly, read like a telephone directory, like Rabbie Burns, like Pavarotti, like Adolf Hitler, like Alastair Burnett, read blandly, hysterically, with dignity, warmth, compassion, sensitivity. But never did I hear it cried out of the centre of chaos, for the sake of an eternal principle, that if we were worth dying for, He is worth being broken for.

In other words, the breaking of the bread is meaningless, pointless, is a non-reality, if He is not there Himself. And if He is there, we must attend to what it is that we are doing. And that, in certain circumstances, means pursuing the logic of the theme through whatever discord is required to achieve a harmony which actually has meaning. For without potential discord there is no music, only confectionery. At the end of that service, I was exhausted, as we all were, for it was as if the statue in the cemetery in Don Giovanni had come alive and opened a trapdoor into an ultimate dimension where the choices were real. The liturgy like the statue, had come alive. Jesus was crucified, but He was - perhaps - risen.

Points remain to be made about this. The first is that any attempt, simple or complex, quiet or spectacular, to be true to the deepest reality, to let free that deep magic which is C.S. Lewis's phrase for the nakedly supernatural, is fraught with risk. It is a condition of real artistic management that the material may finish up managing you. Second, in the midst of this turbulence, the most exact description I can give of what I felt inside myself is silence. I was transported into an area of seriousness from which all triviality was excluded. If music, words, actions, liturgy, faith, could be this serious, then there was nothing left to say.

Third, you don't have to share the Whitley view of liturgy, of communion, even of Christ, to allow the general point that whatever your hunch about a matter of religion, art, or life, sometimes the only way to back that hunch is to go away over the top. I am a great respecter of those who go over the top, because they are frequently disparaged by the Pharisees of their group, community, or profession, so they go over, more often than not, alone. Yet, not alone, for - fourth - the quiet experiences in the Ardersier country church and the turbulent experience in St. Giles were the same experience, the Easter experience of another being there, of something going on that could not be fully explained by a time and motion study of the events physically and intellectually taking place. Again, this is not a matter for Christians only. All art is about this. If art is not about that Real Presence, it is not art at all. Music is about that 'other', potentially beside and within. Music is about a sometimes frightening, but ultimately friendly universe.

In more recent times, my wife and I attended Easter Sunday morning service in Paisley Abbey. We went there, not for what we thought we might get out of it, but because we wanted to support the minister who in the preceding year had experienced a wife with cancer and the break-up of his marriage. Ministers being goldfish in bowls called Manses, everyone in the congregation was fully apprised of all this. The atmosphere in the packed Abbey had, therefore, a certain frisson. Being the Abbey, the music under George McPhee was of great distinction. The minister being Johnston McKay the prayers and sermon were of an equal distinction. All that was inspiring enough. What made the occasion breath-taking was the sense of the bread of truth being broken. The preacher's voice appeared to break on at least one occasion, yet the urgency of his kerugmatic and pastoral message was not sentimentalised. As a result, the singing of choir, and especially of congregation broke through Scottish reserve. There was a sensation of rising, rising through and rising above, pain, defeat, and all the big and little deaths of our lives. Having gone to support, we came away supported. There had been another Presence there. The grace to be vulnerable had transmuted into the courage to be: and this had alchemised the service from being a memorial to an Easter of long, long ago into being a new Easter, here, now.

Of the enchanted buildings whose doors have admitted my entry to liturgical other worlds, none is more famous than Durham Cathedral and none more infamous in our times than its bishop. On the Easter weekend of 1988, I was in York on film business. Having spent the Good Friday vigil in York Minster,

I had an impulse early on the Sunday morning to bowl up the A1 to attend the Matins and Communion Services at Durham. Both services turned out to be inspirational musically and kerugmatically. The then Dean at the first, and the Bishop at the second, preached with clarity and fire. When three months later I lay in intensive care fighting for the survival of a cardiac system that was trying to obey genetic instructions to despatch me, the remembered clasp of the Bishop of Durham's hand as he handed me the wafer was among those weapons that won for me another round of life.

It was therefore in a mood of grateful pilgrimage that the following Easter I climbed up the hill to the same two services in Britain's most sublime Norman building. But there was acid in the air. That very morning, the Bishop had surfaced as headline news. Yet again he was held to be denying the actuality of Christ's resurrection. His alleged apostasy was all over the Sunday papers. (The Easter Monday editorials in quality papers were even heavier in judgement). I had little doubt, as was later confirmed, that he had been set up by the media to provide an Easter story, but I was still perturbed. David Jenkins used a limited openness of language to reformulate eternal truths - 'always reforming' being a Reformation principle; was such theological activity now fair game not only for the lynch mob of journalists, but for apoplectic politicians and dyspeptic churchmen?

Twenty-four hours later, Jenkins recovered his resilience, but as he climbed the pulpit steps to preach he seemed vulnerable, and indeed his voice broke near the end. What you cannot mistake, after a lifetime of church attendance, is atmosphere. I was surrounded by a thousand people who were on the edges of their mental seats. The sermon was four things: witty - the funny asides drew that kind of instant response only obtainable from an audience that is with you; exegetically serious; eschatologically urgent (the theme was that God has raised Jesus from the dead to judge us at the end of all things); and, at its climax, evangelically emotive in its confession of belief. This address was not *about* resurrection. It *was* resurrection. That, the vast congregation made clear, in the warmth with which every one of the them was determined to shake the Bishop's hand at the door.

All this, however, for present purposes is but background to the musical happening. The sound of that throng singing the Easter hymns with the support of the organ in full throat was, from the outset, never short of wonderful. After the sermon, however, there was a sea-change. The Cathedral organist, James Lancelot, finished with conducting the choir downstairs, nipped up to the organ loft. There are a number of explanations of what followed. It is possible that the Assistant Organist had laid by in the loft a crate of malt whisky, some casks of Amontillado, or even just a bottle of claret, and that the final hymns and voluntary were played upside down by their four feet, their right hands being busy toasting the Bishop with a glass or two, while their left hands threw incendiary devices into the *Tuba Mirabilis*. Or, enthused by end of term Easteritis, they were jumping up and down on trampolines attached to the manual keyboards and pedals. The only flaw in these otherwise persuasive scenarios is that the wildness of the emotional conflagration was expressed in playing of such brilliance that what burned off the walls of the nave and lifted the central tower into orbit was not grotesque noise but glorious music. What it expressed was: the grave is open. The congregation lifted into orbit with it. That roar of a multitude transfigured by love into an epiphany swirled around the stone arches before flying through the hole where the tower had been. The tumult went rolling over the fields of England and the Pennine hills to Southwick's pearl of a church in a little clearing in the trees, where these days by the Solway I find a special silence, up over the crowns of St. Giles, and Paisley Abbey, and down into the graveyard by the Moray Firth where Ardersier Church used to stand. There, the sound went wherever it is that sounds go when they die. It was the end of all things indeed; but this was an eschaton where the last trump was happy. I have no doubt that the Jenkins sermon, rising out of its context of a beleaguered, partly broken preacher, raised all of us there that day, and that the Cathedral organist, caught up existentially in that breakage and resurrection, lifted us into an apogee. Speaking subjectively, at the crowning climax of the last hymn, with tears on not my face only, what I heard in my heart was not any sound at all, but the wonder of an absolute silence.

You know how it is when you come out of the cinema. You have been absorbed in a world, and suddenly you're back in the other one of streets, busy pavements, bus queues, rain, or even more disorientating, sunlight. As we emerge from the liturgical 'highs' I have described, we should perhaps look in sober daylight at a couple of potential *caveats* to all I have been saying, and the way I've been saying it.

The first may seem tendentious, not to say trivial; but it might be as well for me to say it before someone thinks it. I've been using a certain kind of language to express experiences which I would describe as spiritual. Others would say they were merely emotional. Others again would be more precise. Raking about in their Freudian dustbins, they would point out that the language I used to describe climaxes of excitement in St. Giles and Durham was not a million miles from the kind of prose that might be deployed by an excitable novelist to describe - well, you know, the kind of thing which used to be covered in the cinema by crashing waves and cameras angling up to the sky. Now, of course, you, and you, and you, would never entertain such a thought, but over there, behind the pillar... so let me just deal with it. Although Freud's simplistic, if not downright distorted tunnel vision into the unconscious is now as vulnerable as Newton's view of a mechanical universe, the trickle down of its assumptions has affected popular thinking, and lies, I suspect, behind some of the latent scepticism about religion and liturgy in our secular culture.

For example, theological students have told me they are too embarrassed to sing certain devotional hymns because of the supposed psychological naïvety of the author. One specifically mentioned was John Newton's 'How Sweet the Name of Jesus Sounds', with Freudian toes particularly curling over the verse, 'Jesus, my Shepherd, Husband, Friend'. Gosh, how awkward, to have old Sigmund up there in the rafters, lasering into our subconscious, to report neurotic defects to - well, to whom?

Does God mind? This is on the verge of being such rubbish that one is inclined to dismiss it. But, as I shall keep saying, if we are to recover our emotional nerve in the matter of church music, then we have to recover it on a broad front, and not be forced on to the defensive on matters emotional, for without emotion music is worth zilch.

We'll return to this general question again. Just to dispose of the psychoanalytical twitchers, let me say that the great central tower of Durham Cathedral is not only a phallic symbol, it is also, by happy chance, the great central tower of Durham Cathedral; and the Usher and McEwan Halls, where I describe other climactic experiences, are not only, being round, conceivably (it's not very likely, but I'm making a case) suggestive of those pleasant objects referred to in the Song of Solomon in a number of lyrical ways, they are also, in the real world I inhabit, the Usher Hall and the McEwan Hall. When God composed His Creation, He integrated it in such a way that an infinite number of micro and macro elements mirror each other in harmony and counterpoint. Those who seek to undermine the open experience and expression of spiritual uplift by recourse to psychological formulae achieve either what George McLeod has often referred to with pardonable exasperation as 'analysis paralysis', or, more likely, *reductio ad absurdum*.

There is, however, a more serious point to be attended to.

That is that a substantial number of people would say that everything I've been saying so far is absolute codswallop. Many trained in philosophy, linguistics and music would think that my use of language has been sloppy to the point of distorting all the categories that make rigorous inter-disciplinary dialogue meaningful, that my whole word and world view is hopelessly romantic and out of date, and that my anecdotal approach to the subject is worthy of a coffee table compendium of children's addresses, but not of a serious approach to the aesthetic and practical problem of church music.

To hear this said would be wonderfully reassuring, suggesting that possibly I am, after all, on the right lines. Not because they are wrong and I am right, but because in this matter there is no right or wrong, only the freedom to be true to one's experience. Language should not be an army to deploy defensively or aggressively against a foe. That is what Jesus had to contend with as the scribes and Pharisees tried to box Him in. Language is a door to open. But I recognise that such criticism levelled against my approach would be entirely justified on its terms. What it would say would be in essence a direct rebuttal. Where I say music is much wider than sound patterns, it is a way of listening to the cosmos, and by implication, of finding meaning there, they would say the whole point of music is to be meaningless: it is just notes. It is not a transferable experience. They would possibly say the same of poetry, certainly of painting. The visual experience is itself. It is not 'about' something else.

I respect that view and the rigour of the analysis that protects it. But in my assessment all that does is to push the meaning argument one stage back. If music is only notes, why do we bother, for example, to spend millions of pounds to build the new Glasgow Royal Concert Hall?

But I am happy to answer the point with one phrase of the so recently departed Leonard Bernstein. Speaking not theoretically, but as a master magician in the arena of practical music making, he once said, "Music is a metaphor for living."

At the beginning of this chapter, I compared religious music, first to a cool summer drink, then to a warming winter cuppa. I then said water is actually what we need to survive at all; and some form of non-linear expression, such as music, is as essential for the spiritual life as water is for the physical. I finish however, with wine. What goes with the broken bread is spilled wine. What flows in our veins and is pumped by our heart to give us a full bodied life is blood. In the end, music that is not full-blooded is dead. I hope I have said enough to show that to be full-blooded is not necessarily to be loud, or big, or quiet, or this, or that, or anything. It is just to be alive. We may not be here for a purpose. We may be meaningless fragments amidst the shards of the stars. But, even so, each of us has the vocation, however hidden, to pick up sparkles from the star that made us, those sparkles that move in our veins and surface in electrical impulses in our brains. And I hope you can see that these sparkles hidden within us all make up the music of our life. That is our life. Our life is, or is meant to be, music.

In the film 'On The Beach', as the lonely submarine passed on a Sunday morning though the Golden Gate, San Francisco lay around, untouched by bombs, but dead, silent. Except for one sound. A radio signal in morse. Though the lifeless streets the American submariners traipsed, desperate to meet just one human survivor. When found, it was discovered to be a bit of morse apparatus operating on its own. That was sound, but not music. Powerful though it is, that is not the Christian myth. We say something else. Music is not gilt on the gingerbread. It is the metal that does not corrupt, stored against the recession of light, health, mortal breath. Music appears to end in silence. But as we pass through the gate of that silence, out of that non-mythical furnace from which all myths come we will hear something - not an undecodable message tapped out by a dead universe, but that which makes the divine human and the human divine: an ultimate music, a good magic - trustworthy alchemy - a voice of redeemable and redeeming gold.

Chapter Four

THE SIXTH GOLD RING

I began Chapter Three by describing the seminal effect of a cold drink on a hot day and a hot drink on a cold one, these being sensual analogies to the effect of music on worship and life. I would like to press that analogy into further service.

Take an empty chilled church. Drop in a couple of clergy in vestments - clunk, clunk. Now take a liturgy well matured in prayer books and pour into the stained glass. Glug, glug. Now comes the moment you've been waiting for all week. Lift yourself off the kneeler and imbibe the liturgy slowly. Maybe it's more solid fare you're after. So go down the road for a Presbyterian loaf. Slice with CH3, or other hymn book. Take a tub of low-voltage Bible spread made from extracts of Old and New Testaments in modern middle-management English. Now reach for a jar of potted news paste and spread thinly. Finally, sprinkle on some references to last night's TV, and serve on a hard pew. Still hungry and thirsty? What you need is a pick me up. Here is a bottle of nourishing charismatic juice, made up from the healthiest ingredients - shining faces, clapping hands, swinging music, a high Jesus content, and those extra vitamins your emotions need - kissing, hugging and healing. Shake vigorously with the Holy Spirit, close your eyes, and drink without stopping to think.

All lies. Well, clichéd pastiche. The truth is more subtle. Any form of worship is a jug of water. Water, as we said, is necessary for life. The interesting question is: what special presence may turn that water into wine? What turns communication into communion? But even more interesting: what kind of special presence might that be? Behind the question of what form we give our worship lies the primeval question: what is the divine like? Is God showbiz - clown, actor-manager, movie star; or is He politician or president; or is He theologian, author, reformer, executive, judge?

We aren't likely to get very far with that question, but because I believe it lurks behind much unconscious prejudice about worship, I'd like to explore it down one avenue. Before doing so, I'd better explain why I won't explore it down another avenue which might seem obvious, namely, the Jesus of the Gospels avenue. If it is suggested that we know what God is like by seeing what Jesus is like, I have to ask: which Jesus? Showbiz rears its head here also, because our modern images of Jesus are not delivered to our brain straight from the reality of Palestine two thousand years ago. We have seen the part acted on TV and film. There are as many kinds of Jesus in our brain as there are actors who have played Him; but also as there are preachers who have preached Him, hymn writers who have hymned Him, and feminists who are now 'her'ring Him.

The avenue I would like to go down for a moment is, as usual, by analogy. In The Quest TV series, David Jenkins described God as "an unstoppable artist". Taking one kind of artist as a focus, imagine God as an orchestral conductor. Of course there are a zillion ways in which God is not like a conductor, but there are a couple of ways in which He might just be. Here are sixty or ninety rampant individualists - as musicians are - all doing their own thing... I mean, would you try to arrange a marriage between a flute and a trombone? Admittedly, a trombone and a tuba might be worse. I once shared a student flat with an oboeist and that was bad enough. Yet this potential anarchy has to be led into glorious unanimity. Compare the cacophony of the tuning up with the first chord of the concert. How does that radical alteration occur? Could this be the special presence that turns water into wine? It has to be a very special presence, for it is essential that the unanimity is not enforced by mechanical tyranny. If the musicians do not retain their creative freedom the sound is strained, metallic or scrawny; or the opposite, over-suave. In a word, it is sound, not music. Even when the orchestral blend is acoustically succu-lent, a lack of spontaneity in the orchestra can undermine the essence of what the composer is saying. Great music carries within itself the same contradiction between freedom and order, resolved by a magic we call art or inspiration or genius.

Karajan was incapable of making an orchestra sound unbeautiful, but to my mind the freedom of the music was hostage to that perfection. The Karajan sound had that quality of ultimate glutinosity which is the musical equivalent of the concept of Heaven as a cosmic soup, a condition in which all our rugged individuality is subsumed into a oneness even more boring, because longer lasting, than the ecumenical movement. But lest I should sound dismissive of Herbert von Karajan on the one hand, or the Very Reverend von MacTavish-Hustleburger on the other, let me say, again on the drinking plane, that I defend to the death the right of every free-drinking Scotsman, Englishman, Irishman and Japaneseman to take on board a comforting wee dram of the perfectly blended ecumenical hard stuff, appropriately mixed with organisational water, while preferring myself, as an only occasional quaffer of the staff of life, to let an individualistic malt like Macallan of Speyside or Bowmore of Islay declare its soul directly to my palate. In tune with the glory of Scots malts, I offer you two conductors who offered to their musicians a freedom which I feel in my bones reflected the divine readiness to take risks.

The first was Thomas Beecham. I'm not claiming him as a democrat. He was a tyrant, if ever I saw one. But he was a very funny tyrant. And once, like Spike Milligan, another funny tyrant, you allow the rogue elephant of humour into the china shop of ideas, you give up the one thing that makes tyranny despicable and diabolical: totalitarian control. The other element in the Beecham tyranny was humility. No, it's not a silly paradox. Since the days of antiquity, people have dreamed of the philosopher-king, who would use power to liberate minds and spirits. We referred to this concept when we considered the awful power-potential of the pipe organ. Beecham placed his genius for high voltage command at the disposal of the music, the muse, the mystery, the miracle.

But enough rhetoric. Let me describe an occasion. I was in the Usher Hall organ gallery once when Beecham conducted the Royal Philharmonic. After the interval he breasted the stairs and penetrated the platform door like a plenipotentiary capercaillie. He navigated the thicket of music stands and fiddle players and advanced on the podium. A bow of quite unnecessary depth to the bourgeoisie in the stalls accomplished, he turned and surveyed the orchestra. Although he had been with them throughout the first half, his wicked eyes raked them like a submarine periscope surveying an unexpected battle fleet. He turned to the orchestral leader and enquired with mild curiosity,

"What are we going to play now?"

"Brahms Two", said First Violin McCallum, trained not to giggle.

"Oh good", said Tommy Beecham, "I know that one."

With an air of some satisfaction, he picked up the score from the desk, dropped it on the floor, and nonchalantly began beating his stick. In a relaxed sort of way, the orchestra joined in and played the first movement. The slow movement of Brahms' Second is generally described as "sunny" by programme note writers who predated the discovery that sun causes cancer. It opens on the strings. Without warning, Beecham swooped upon them like an enraged vulture. Talons tearing at their breasts, he sawed away at their vitals. It was a cross between 'The Rite of Spring' and World War Three. The Usher Hall moved several yards down Lothian road. Having achieved both magnificence and war, he then seemed to fall half asleep and conducted the third movement with an abstracted air. There was a pause before the last movement. He squared his shoulders. "Right," he barked, "tally-ho," and they were off. His baton was a whip, the orchestra were the hounds of Hell after the cosmic fox. He cheered on the final pages which got faster and faster. The audience was on its feet baying while the brass fanfares were still braying. It may or may not have been exactly what Brahms meant, but it was sublime entertainment.

Another year, I saw Furtwängler conduct the very same symphony, and it was merely sublime. He was then old, a gaunt skeletal fibroid. He brooded over the orchestra as the hall waited in an expectation which was almost tangibly painful.

Then the arm came down with that famous beat, a vague motion out of whose fluttering ambiguity the orchestra had the freedom to choose the moment to begin. Out of caverns of Hell the horns called, and a mournful sound eased into life. Compared to Beecham's sunny opening, this was like the skeletons of Buchenwald rattling out of the jaws of death. Yet, paradoxically, the slow movement which Beecham had turned into Apocalypse Now, Furtwängler played as sunnily as Julie Andrews having an afternoon stroll up the Alps.

Which was Brahms, Beecham or Furtwängler? Neither, and both. In each case a genius opened gates through which a universe travelled to be born: a universe of which Brahms was one parent.

Perhaps God is like that. Well, at least partly like that: an unpredictable creative genius who triggers possibilities; one of the progenitors of every birth; for the truth about the Virgin Birth may be not that only one birth was virgin, but that in a sense, every birth, biological, and artistic is. Every new beginning is that: a truly new beginning. But God encompasses both the hilarious entertainer and the tragic progenitor. Music includes the light and the dark, Christmas and Good Friday, Easter and Harvest. God is a sufficiently versatile showbiz manager that He lets it all show. Does that mean God has no taste, no preference? Is He even interested? Or, to put it this way, is God musical? Do we have music in church because it pleases God or because it pleases us? If God is not musical, why are we bothering? If He is, along what lines should we be bothering? Is God for Brahms, Wagner, Mozart, or Bach? And does He like them dished up by a Beecham or a Furtwängler? And in church music terms, does He go for Poulenc or... or... or for Twentieth Century religious light music?

Now, why did I hesitate there? Suppose, all these centuries, God has hated the pipe organ? Who's been listening, then, to all these church Evensong voluntaries? Alternatively, has He these past thirty years been clapping His hands to His ears every time a guitar group has stationed itself on the chancel steps? Or, horror of horrors, has He been clapping His hands enthusiastically in time to the beat?

The only reason you're not bothering to tell me this is anthropomorphic nonsense is that it is so obviously anthropomorphic nonsense. But hold your horses. Suppose I say to you that obviously God will prefer good music to bad music, that He is bound to prefer a polished cathedral choir to a rough parish one, that a great hymn will of course please Him more than a locally produced tune. Or that serious composers like Bach, Palestrina, Herbert Howells, Kenneth Leighton and Martin Dalby are obviously going to afford Jehovah a more lively aesthetic satisfaction than Stainer's oratorical equivalents of 19th Century stained glass, John Bell's drumming up of Scots-African wild geese on Iona, or Ian Mackenzie's improvised hymnological cocktails on Radio Scotland. You will fly into an absolutely justified theological rage and say that God is not an élitist, not an aesthete, not a musical Pharisee: He judges, not by an aesthetic standard, but by the purity of the heart. Let a person, a choir, a congregation, sing a song, however aesthetically poor, with radiant sincerity, and that is worth more to the Father of our crucified Lord than all the authentically recorded Baroque cantatas in Leipzig.

If, however, you rebut the assertion that God cares for high musical standards by the counter-assertion that He cares for something else - moral motive, emotional integrity, spiritual single-mindedness, or whatever - this is still an anthropomorphic assessment. God, you are implying, is listening and saying, "Here in St. X.s Cathedral is a splendid piece of music, but I prefer in St. Y's Church that indifferent performance of that awful piece of music because the performers mean well - there's heart in it." Is this not rather like a critic reviewing the first night of a new musical and applying warm-hearted Shaftesbury Avenue showbiz criteria rather than Broadway critical surgery? And what's wrong with that? Nothing, unless you object to anthropomorphic criteria in the area of God: which, a moment ago in objecting to musical élitism, you did.

It looks like we can't escape from this doublebind, because we have anthropomorphic minds. We are human, and human characteristics make up our reference grid.

But, guess what... the way out is provided by the very music we were scrutinising. The truth is not that we judge the music. The truth is that it judges us, in the sense of seeking us out. Moreover, we do not judge the music in relation to God from some abstract position. God, if He is there at all, judges us *via* the music. If He's not there, then of course we are free to consider only aesthetic judgements. But if God is there, He comes to us in the music - as well as in other things, like words, images, and people. It is not that we have to find a way to God by choosing the right music. It is that God makes music right for us.

But - possibly under certain conditions. And possibly sincerity is not the only condition. To say God doesn't care about the music is possibly to patronise Him and diminish ourselves. To identify something called a heart which operates independently of mind and ear may be to diminish the complexity of God's own creation and to diminish the human spirit's own achievements in its thinking, singing, and playing voyage towards the unknown.

Why am I muddying the already brackish waters of the problems of church music by bringing in abstract questions about God? Surely these lectures are designed to be helpful, not theoretical. Yes, but what in the long run is helpful? Practical solutions to practical questions must be found on the ground, in each location, by practical people facing their practical problems. There is now an active Committee of the General Assembly, which is increasingly in touch with practical experiments in Scottish parishes. The Baird Lecture Series, being every five years, offers an opportunity to stand back as far as possible and look at underlying questions. And there are profound underlying questions lurking in the church music debate. The fundamental split, it seems to me, is between the verticals and the horizontals.

The most obvious evidence of the conflict is between the supposed old guard and the young bloods. I think too much is made of this. There is of course an inevitable and natural manifestation of the generation gap which is seen in all areas of church and secular life. Certainly, the pipe organ and the traditional church choir lie across a chasm of taste and fashion from a rock group, or even a folk and guitar group. But there is more to it than this. What is at stake here is not any specific burning bush; if there is a pillar of fire, it does not stand in any one camp or lead any one category of camp followers. It is not the case that so-called evangelicals, fundamentalists, or charismatics are more in the vertical force field than so-called liberals or high-church formalists. Nor vice-versa. I know evangelicals who are for ever talking in vertical language about a risen Jesus and the Spirit, but who would drop down dead with astonishment if God actually did something that wasn't predicted in their theology, or covered by their biblical vocabulary; this unpreparedness for surprises marks them out as actual horizontals, and I know liberals who are for ever talking in terms of horizontal community and political issues but are daily expecting miracles. They are effectively verticals. And I know of a wide spectrum of permutations in between these extremes.

What I am really talking about here is an awareness of, and readiness for, danger. And here I dare to introduce a category which may baffle, bewilder, bemuse, or even be offensive: magic. At the practical level - yes, I stress, practical level - music is nothing, gets nowhere, does not even start from anywhere, if magic is not involved. But also at the theoretical, theological level, there is in my book no place for music in religion or in church if it is not there to cast a spell. For my music book is a spell book, not a spelling book; a spellbinding book, not a book of binding texts in black binding. I'm talking about the dazzling white magic of Christmas, Epiphany, Candlemas, and Easter Sunday, the wild red magic of Pentecost, the golden waving magic of Harvest blending into the dark brown magic of winter, where burnished trombones yield to the silver trumpets on the midnight Advent battlements. All this is the force of real magic - and what it is ranged against is not the absence of force, but the presence of a hostile force, the anti-magic or black magic of bible-black dogma, piety-encrusted sentimentality, and a secular humanist rejection of the supernatural. This rejection of the supernatural is based on outdated 19th Century Newtonian physics, but it frequently masquerades as a Gospel-based, community action programme, motivated by sociologically aware, real Christianity, as compared to what it would portray as out of date *mumbo-jumbo* practised by arty-crafty élitist dinosaurs.

I just want magic to rule OK - and I believe that it can, in virtually any musical language and with almost any degree of music resource. Magic, I believe, comes to those who live dangerously. In alternative words, risk is all. What it boils down to is in what I said in the last chapter: go over the top. I do not mean, make a show of going over the top. I mean: really go over the top. It's not a question of, "Is danger good for you?" It is the fundamental as distinct from the fundamentalist state of affairs that danger is all that there is, once you break through the carapace of whatever gives you superficial comfort. The ultimate is-ness of being alive is, from beginning to end, a project of peril. Music is the perception of that peril at one level of sensibility. All you can do is throw yourself off the cliff, not of a principle, but of a possibility. As both George MacLeod and Harry Whitley said - they were so close, it is impossible to disentangle the source of this or that aphorism - if you drop enough bricks, you can build something with them. But let me not suggest that 'danger' is a gimmick. It isn't a trifling thing, a melodramatic gesture, a cartoon of Batman *ex machina*. Danger is at the heart of existence.

Danger at the heart of church music? Danger at the heart of the church? Imagine the quietest, safest venue in the world - an English cathedral on a darkening winter afternoon, around the time for Evensong. Danger at its heart? In 'Murder In The Cathedral', T.S. Eliot spells out that there is no safety in the Cathedral. In his evocation of the land and the people waiting between golden October and sombre November, you can hear the organ pedal throb alternating hope and despair in the cycle of the years. In the case of Canterbury, it was real murder. And across the world in our own time, cathedrals have throbbed to real martyrdom, real blood spilled, real hopes crucified, and sometimes the blossoming of real freedom. Thus T.S. Eliot, the austere intellectual, the élitist, waspish, aesthetic Anglican, speaks for us all about the pain of waiting for the Kingdom. And in that is a lesson: that humanity is a blood vessel connecting us all. On the edge of the prairie of stars, what matter if we are professors or farmers, poets or primary teachers, brilliant church organists or pianistic performers of eightsome reels pressed into service on the organ stool? We are the human family ranged against the dark.

Well, shall the Son of Man be born again in what Eliot calls the litter of scorn? In the poverty of what we actually have in the average Scottish parish - dull singing, a less than brilliant organist, a minister or priest hard-pressed by a thousand commitments, a people who may feel: here is no action, yet they hold their souls intact, ready to wait and witness - what is the *dénouement* to be?

As you will have perceived by now, my intuitive response to a difficult matter is not so much a theory as an anecdote; for in an anecdote is at least some reality - the reality of human life; whereas logical theory is a rarified form of poetry which may or may not relate to life. I wish therefore to introduce you anecdotally to some people who to my certain knowledge waited and witnessed to some effect. I have to use the past tense because their planetary witness has, in biological terms, ended. They are, assessed statistically, dead. In my brain, however, they are perpetually alive, and that is partly because they lived eschatologically; that is, they were waiting, in their busy lives, for the last things. To put it another way, they waited upon ultimate matters. The Christian witness is of this kind, and in this it is like the artist's or musician's witness; not waiting passively for the next day, or the next event, or, at the end, for the next life, but running to meet reality with an alert readiness which sometimes seems impatient.

My first witness exhibited this impetuous impatience in a marked degree. His name was Erik Routley. He started life as son of the Mayor of Brighton, and he finished it, lamentably early, as Professor of Church Music at Princeton, but for most of his life he was in Britain, an academic in Oxford, then a pastor in Edinburgh and Newcastle, becoming President of the Congregational Union. He was a musician and a composer, but his singular distinction lay in the fact that he was an authentic musical theologian. That is a rare bird, and none so rare as Erik. His grasp of moral and theological principles in the aesthetic field was uniquely lucid. But that sounds sober. The magic thing about Erik was his hilarity. When he laughed he didn't just, *à la* Wodehouse, make a noise like a paper bag bursting. He jumped into the air. He stamped his feet. He shouted. He barked. It seemed at such times that the world was safe with God, because God was shouting and laughing and jumping. Erik Routley had elements of Chesterton without the paradoxical coat-trailing, Falstaff without the grossness, Wesley without the rhetoric, and Luther without the constipation. Erik Routley was a sizzler. His written prose sizzled. When he spoke it was with sizzling energy. The piano or organ keys sizzled when he hit them. However, what sizzled most significantly was his sense of truth. For him the criterion for music was truth and the criterion for church music was theological truth. Many kinds of theology and art claim to be truthful. Routley's criteria, however, convinced me. Three of them are relevant in this context. I will sketch them briefly.

First, music either does or does not carry authority. If it doesn't, it is bad music. Good church music carries moral or theological authority.

Second, however, it is also of the essence of Christian music to be disposable, because our posture is *vis-à-vis* eternity. Against the desert of infinity, we are dwellers in tents. We are travellers and must be ever ready to lift our cultural tents for pitching in a new place. So - we should junk music that no longer works. Clearly, this means that whatever the authority of good Christian music is based on, it cannot be the weight of status or tradition or the intensity with which it takes itself solemnly. Rejecting the boringly slipshod, sentimental, and pompous does not mean rejecting the interestingly temporary, humble, simple or amateur.

Third, and critically, Christian truth comes sideways. The essence of Jesus' teaching lies in parables. That is a form of communicating in which truth is not placed securely in your hand in a safely bound parcel, but is thrown into the air in an arc, a parabola, which you may or may not catch. There is a built-in risk that you may not catch it. This leaves you with your freedom. Routley had much more to say and has said it in several books. These insights, however, stamp him in my mind as having identified better than anyone that church music is a gloriously risky dancing partner in life and worship, yet worth pursuing and wooing with persistence; and conversely, that while Christian music is, if it is authentic, authorised by a God of Truth who may discriminate stringently between bone and marrow, it is invigorated by a Spirit of Adventure which should add greatly to the *hilaritas* of the nations.

We may take it, then, that authority does not lie in sobriety. Our archetypal author, God, is not as sober as a judge. He is as experimentally hellbent on hilarity as a child. How could anyone totally sober create the Big Bang, the Universe, us? Does this contradict what I said in Chapter Three about finding music sometimes so serious that one can be awestruck into inner silence and think it impossible to laugh again? You bet your bottom dollar it contradicts it. I had these solemn thoughts when I was in my late teens, the time for spots, calf love, and lying awake all night pondering the meaning of it all. Well, I still lie awake all night pondering the meaning of it all, I still have calf love every time I see a newborn calf. Only my spots have cleared. But I can now see the joke about seriousness. I can now see that I was so intensely serious, so intoxicated by solemnity, that there was a kind of *hilaritas* about the seriousness. It was certainly not a dull time. And there were two things I never doubted: that God had a sense of humour, even if sometimes it was of the gallows variety; and that He was a master of showbiz. As the greatest entertainer of all time, with extensive commitments in Infinity, He takes some beating: look around you at the sky at night, or at the riotous assembly of flora, fauna and Jock Tamson's Bairns assembled on Sauchiehall Street by day.

"Let Glasgow flourish by the preaching of the word", is the proud Glasgow motto. The operative word is flourish. Glasgow is great at flourishes: Garden Festivals, cultural bonanzas, crazy balloon pageants, Mayfest community street theatre, Jessye Norman in the new Royal Concert Hall, ebullient buskers in Buchanan Street, magic in George Square. Music is, you could say, the *Logos*, the word in a state of flourishment. Music is the word throwing its hat into the ring, into the air. Throwing a hat into the ring is not merely a metaphor. When my son Stephen was baptised in the Muckle Kirk of Peterhead, it was Pentecost. Thousands of red paper tongues were dropped from the gallery, Harry Whitley, who was presiding, danced an eightsome reel in front of the communion table with some children, and a male dancer did a terrific Irish jig, at the end of which he threw his green cap into the congregation. All of this was reasonably hilarious, but I believe it was also truthful, as a varied exegesis of the scriptures for that day, in which the disciples were alleged to have been drunk.

Hilaritas is therefore not an easy option. It is a choice we make. Jesus is reported as saying: when you fast, when you're going through a rigorous process of self-discipline, for reasons ascetic, aesthetic, or athletic, don't make a meal of it as the scribes and pharisees, the professional martyrs, do. Kid everyone you're the top of the morning. Have a ball. Put make up on. Cavort, chortle, chirrup. Well, it's easier said than done. One Easter I was in charge of the music on Iona for a theological students' conference. On Easter Monday morning, when I went to play the piano for the early service, I felt awful. I hadn't slept, there had been a celebratory bibulation the night before, and my perspective on the world was shaded grey black to black with knobs on. I approached the task in hand with the enthusiasm of a hungover hamster facing an early morning jog on the wheel. However there was a task in hand and it was to play music appropriate to Easter Monday. George MacLeod prayed prayers sparkling like a spring burn in spate, the sun shone, and Jesus was risen. So - my playing would have to rise, whatever I felt like. My voluntary at the end was, therefore, a light cascade of sequences on the Easter hymn, the rhythm was a light dancing one.

Afterwards I met George striding down the nave. He appraised me as if I was something the cat had dragged in, and growled, "Just because you feel like a kitten on the keys this morning, doesn't mean the rest of us have to be subjected to flippancy." Clearly, I wasn't the only one feeling liverish. But neither of us had let the liver dictate the liturgical mood. So, yes, the liturgy of life has to be worked at, if it is to rise like a soufflé, and if there is to be life in the liturgy, that choice has to be made, even if it is against the grain. And making that choice is always spiced with unpredictable perils. We stay on Iona for my next witness to the dangers of waiting on the eschatological edge of worship. This witness's name was Ralph Morton.

Waiting is the operative word. I have been waiting for half a lifetime to pay tribute to this man. His posture was a waiting one, not in a passive sense, but an Advent one. In a posture of alert impatience, this largely unrecognised apostle maintained an eschatological witness. He was aware of the last things beating at the window of daily chores; but, unlike angelic preachers, he did not parade his awareness by orating highly coloured commercials for the angels. Ralph Morton attended to the chores: of which for two summers on Iona I was one, in my capacity as Music Director to the Abbey and the Youth Camps. I bring Ralph Morton in here for he is a cardinal witness to my thesis that church music is not an area of exclusive interest to musicians. Ralph, you see, was tone deaf. He could not sing. When he tried to, what emanated from his creased face was a drone not metaphorically but literally mono-tonous. Yet from this man, who was guilty of a musical incapacity so massive as to defy the laws of aesthetic gravity, I received a degree of sympathetic comprehension of what music in worship is for that I have received from few others. He lacked, in the most definitive degree possible, a musical ear, yet he was gifted in that other area to which from time to time I refer: he had ears to hear. If his outer musical ear was a Lada, his other, inner ear was a Porsche.

I will adduce two pieces of evidence. As Deputy Leader of the Community, Ralph's multiple tasks included leadership roles in training and study programmes, and in administration. His intellectual capability and pastoral awareness made him formidable in these matters, but it was in his responsibility for the planning of worship that I had constant contact with him. Without (to put it mildly) Erik Routley's musicianship, he nevertheless had Routley's radar capacity for seeking integrity and falseness in music as in words. A hymn could be anathema to him because one line of one verse was theologically weak or rang politically or ethically false, and certain tunes lay under heavy suspicion because a phrase struck him as vacuous, bombastic, or sentimental. I hardly ever disagreed with him, but when I did, he would wryly trade one of his anathemas for one of mine.

My other piece of evidence is more startling. It was difficult in a grandly austere Abbey to find music suitable for a piano, even a grand one. The choice seemed to lie between sounding like a predictably Baroque typewriter or a Palm Court melody machine. I therefore tended to improvise. The musical results may have been doubtful, but I took the process seriously to the extent of trying to weave the 'Word' content of the service into the hymn or psalm tunes used. Ralph Morton listened to these spasmodic utterances and often commented on them in a way which revealed that he followed the musical argument. But one Sunday when I played a particularly complex improvisation lasting half an hour, I was bowled over when he gave me a blow by blow account of how my mind had worked and what theological points I was making.

The paradox in the situation is that George MacLeod spoke affectionately but witheringly of Ralph's musicality. George's musicianship ran to loving what he knew - 'Crimond', 'St. George's Edinburgh', and all the other golden oldies which he pictured being sung under the stars by Community members scattered throughout the world from brightest Africa to darkest Greenock, and he defended these stoutly against certain incursions I was making on these traditions in my two summers doing the Iona music. The fact, however, is that George's native musicality, which was prodigious, expressed itself not through music but in words. To hear him pray at the great Sunday communion was to hear Handel's 'Hallelujah Chorus' or Bach's 'Sanctus' transmuted into verbal tapestry and living sculpture; whereas Ralph Morton, the supposedly dry word man, the gravelly, unmusical logical analyst of ethics and theology was tuned into music. He knew how to decode music.

We must, therefore, refuse to be governed by stereotypes. Which of these two was vertical, which horizontal? Both were vertically-oriented people, although Ralph would have hated being described as such, so intense was his commitment to the practical requirements of the here and now. Both men lived dangerously because they were perpetually listening for the inner meaning of worship, and that exposes you to the threat of the unpredictable, the 'other', invading your life. That may be magic. But it may also just be a damned nuisance. As George said, "It isn't the unanswered prayers that is the problem - it is the answered ones."

Well, enough about human musicality. The question was: is God musical?

No, of course not, in the anthropomorphic sense. But His on-board computer must be capable of decoding what we receive and express through music. After all, if God exists, or even if He, in the conventional sense, doesn't, the original coding of the cosmos included a potential for music.

From our point of view, the question is not so much whether God is musical as whether music has a God-like potential? Whether God or the cosmic force is one of its progenitors. And my answer is, yes! For when the god, or goddess, within us all has spoken, there comes that moment when speech, however lyrical, fails to express what we feel, what we know. All that is left, then, is to fling your hat in the air, or your five gold rings - and one more ring - for God or the cosmos to catch and throw back into the cauldron of that which is not yet formed: the sixth ring.

But, you ask, where did five, or indeed six, gold rings suddenly appear from? To explain that, I produce my last witness.

He was as English as Ralph Morton was Scottish. Sidney Newman was Professor of Music at Edinburgh when I was a music student there in the Fifties. He was of a mystic West Country Elgarian temper, and sometimes it was a temper. He was a big-minded man, but, as other big-minded men have done, he ran up against an Edinburgh establishment - in this case the

musical establishment that dominated Edinburgh in the days
before Scotland's musical Renaissance - pre Herrick Bunney,
pre Ian Pitt-Watson, pre a permanent national orchestra, pre
Alexander Gibson, pre Scottish Opera, and in his first year or
two, pre Edinburgh Festival. Indeed, Newman was one of
those who joined with the Lord Provost and the Editor of The
Scotsman in supporting Rudolf Bing's madcap idea of drown-
ing in festivalitis a city as musically dry as Tio Pepé. Sidney
Newman's predecessor in the Edinburgh Music Chair was the
famous Donald Tovey. Tovey hadn't been just a big man, but
an intellectual giant. His published programme notes remain to
this day a bible of musical analysis - you still find them quoted
by contemporary scribblers. Not as racy as Bernard Shaw, not
as bubbly as Neville Cardus, they have a witty tang of their
own, icing on profound analysis and whiplash judgement. To
follow Tovey was a difficult act, specially when his Edinburgh
disciple, amanuensis, and biographer, Mary Grierson had some
hope of the succession. Newman, in the eyes of Tovey's
Edinburgh disciples, just wasn't up to it. They considered this
gauche laddie transferred from a lecturer's post in Newcastle to
be as intellectually lightweight as he was physically rotund,
and, to boot, to be lacking in those genuflecting skills requisite
on incomers who wished to penetrate the evening circle of
sherry, gin, or *vin des vacances*.

Like Ralph Morton and Erik Routley, Professor Newman
could be disconcertingly direct, which some people took to be
rudeness. But he had something to be direct about. He was in
love. In love with life, with music, with his family, and in a Walt
Whitmanesque fashion with the universe. I say Whitmanesque
with feeling, for I still carry around as psychosomatic stigmata
two souvenirs of early pianistic tension: an ulcer which began
in my 19th year, and a habit of gnashing my teeth when I play.
As the music scholar of my year, I became the accompanist to
the university choir which Newman conducted; and the work
to be tackled in my first term was Vaughan Williams' 'Sea
Symphony' set to words by Walt Whitman. My relationship
with the conductor was robust. If in rehearsal I was a mini-
second late in double-guessing where Newman was about to re-

start, he called me to heel with bar numbers like Barbara Woodhouse telling a spaniel to sit. When he expected me to know, before he zapped it to me, that he was going back two pages, not one, I consigned him privately to hell. But on the night, all was forgiven. He was a visionary choral conductor, specially in religious music. When he smiled, his face shone like the sun. At tender climaxes, he painted the sky with wide sweeps of his arms. When we went with him to the dark side of the moon in the 'St. John Passion', Mozart's 'Requiem', or Kodaly's 'Psalmus Hungaricus', his distress engaged our guts.

His own guts were also involved, for regularly before a major performance he would vomit. In non-choral terms he had two handicaps, small hands and an uncharismatic behind. The latter was conspicuous when he conducted an orchestra, for his orchestral conducting was as wince-making as his choral conducting could be winsome. He jabbed at the orchestra in a half-bent posture which was, posterior-wise, audience un-friendly. Yet, in the course of three years at the Music Faculty, I heard from The Reid Orchestra under Newman dozens of unheard Haydn symphonies performed with such gusto that I have never since thought of the genius of Esterhazy as less substantial than Beethoven.

He confessed that the small reach of his hands had pro-foundly frustrated his ambitions, in that the romantic piano repertoire was beyond him. His response was to throw himself into what lay literally to hand. In my hearing he performed Bach's 'Goldberg Variations' by memory, and addressed him-self with such delicacy and ferocity to that vast and, at its end almost Wagnerian, structure, that even the Edinburgh musical establishment applauded the feat of emotional and technical concentration.

So here I am paying tribute to a big romantic man who found himself limited by small hands, and a small orchestra, in what was then musically a small community; and whose response to all these limitations was to throw himself off the cliff of those possibilities rather than to waste time dreaming of what might have been. There was, however, a psychic cost, and for a whole year, while I was there, he endured a nervous breakdown, and so did we. Every day he came to work. He was difficult to live with, that year, but the work never suffered.

I have taken pains to delineate a man living with substantial elements of discomfort, because discomfort is what is experienced by so many who struggle, day in, day out, with the frustrating limitations imposed upon their musical ambitions by the restrictions of inadequate instruments, unsympathetic Kirk Sessions or church councils, unresponsive congregations, or their own technical handicaps. On many an organ stool Icarus quivers, longing to fly to the sun, but confined to a horizontal plane by a relentless Scotch mist.

However, I would not leave you, or Sidney Newman there. I now come to his apotheosis, from which I have drawn the title of this chapter. My conclusion is that there is usually a gap in the fog, a window sometime, somewhere, in the cloudscape. When the mist clears you may see at first only further and even more daunting pillars of cumulus piled higher and higher. But keep flying up there. Do you see that streak of light... a sudden glint of gold? Keep flying.

Sidney Newman's celestial window, so far as I observed it, came at Christmas. He was the host at the University Carol Party. This took place in the McEwan Hall, that extraordinary building whose bathroom resonance made it wildly unsuitable for most musical excursions. I once gave an organ recital in the McEwan Hall, where the exposed pedal passages in the great Bach 'F Major' came rolling round the hall's echo to shake each other warmly by the throat. Virtually any music there finished up sounding like Palestrina with a bad cold. It was in this unlikely venue that Sidney Newman became fully at home in the musical universe at so many of whose hard edges he baulked. Here all was reconciled in warmth, light, colour, fun, and a good deal of chaos. His personality was released; he played Santa Claus. The traditional carols soared in the cathedral acoustic. The quiet ones whispered like the fragrance of freesias. The bucolic ones stamped and blew on their hands. The sublime ones - 'Adeste Fideles', 'Hark The Herald Angels Sing' - rose into the sky like Adonises of Advent riding on clouds towards Heaven's Christmas gate. But all of that can, I daresay, be experienced elsewhere. What was distinctive about this carol party was the childish fun. Sidney adored children. He got them to come out and mill around for the sweet baby carols. But the furious climax of the evening was something quite else. It came in 'The Twelve Days of Christmas'. My job, at the organ, was to keep up with his demotic conducting impulses. In this setting he was as unpredictable as Spike Milligan. But one thing was predictable. When it came to "Five gold rings", the roof came off. I don't mean simply that it was loud. I mean that the McEwan Hall seemed to shift on the *axis mundi*. An alchemy took place. The hall, no, the world unfurled itself like a gigantic gold ball thrown into the air by a cosmic kitten. Sidney, you see, played with that "gold". In the carol, there is a decoration on that word, a little twirl, like carelessly twirling it round your finger. But a simple twirl was not enough here. It was thrown in the air, bounced off the walls, boomeranged round the upper cavities of the hall. And on the last time round in the final verse, it went into orbit. It was no longer the fifth gold ring, but a sixth pirouetting, celestial, ornament. Time was suspended, as though a sixth dimension of musical gold swept into a Seventh Heaven, on to a Cloud Nine, up to a hilarious moment of space-busting glory - and at that moment, Jesus was born.

If we are prepared to make ourselves vulnerable, take risks, become ridiculous, let the heart out of its cage, then it is possible that not Icarus, but the dove of God's childlike muse flies towards the sun. And that if we travel with it we travel safely into the furnace of that love in which we can be reborn. For at least a moment, the age of gold is with us again; and the kingdom has come. Wherever you are, whatever your situation, however modest your circumstances, flying riskily towards that gap in the cloud is, or should be, the function of church music.

Chapter Five

THE AGE OF GOLD

It was, I think, in 1938, that my father, the minister of Fraserburgh Old Parish Church, clambered on to the stage and faced the audience which packed the Playhouse Cinema in that rugged north eastern fishing town. They had just watched the Fraserburgh première of the film 'Sixty Glorious Years'. To my acute embarrassment, my Dad then led the audience in evening prayers. What a gulf lies between that world and ours! Admittedly, it was a special occasion: the opening of a brand new cinema, all green and shiny and, unlike the flea pit down the road, wonderfully perfumed. Moreover, it was the first showing in Fraserburgh of a film in colour. And it was not just any film. It was the epic of Queen Victoria's reign, in which Anna Neagle played the great lady. Even so, can you envisage in our world such a public entertainment ending with worship? Was there any suggestion that The Biggest Hogmanay Party In The World, which began the Glasgow Year of Culture, should end with prayer?

Between that world of the 30's, and our world of the 90's, lie not only the Second World War, the Bomb, and space travel, but fundamental alterations in the ambience of both public entertainment and public worship. Have they been years of improvement in values, or decline - or both - or neither? Are the arenas of entertainment and worship now terminally separated, or are they coming together in new ways my father would not have dreamt of? Which is better - the Golden Age that has gone, or the new Golden Age that is coming?

Sixty years ago, the first - and only other - series of Baird Lectures on church music was given by Dr Wauchope Stewart, minister of St. Mary's, Haddington; and naturally, they were delivered in the language of that more formal age. Were Dr Stewart to be beamed back through sixty years, glorious or otherwise, to the future Scotland of 1990, not only would he find St. Mary's, in its rebuilt form, to be an unfamiliar spectacle; he would hardly recognise much of the church music scene.

But whereas he would surely rejoice over the Lamp of the Lothians' glorious renaissance, it is less certain that he would regard as glorious all that he would now hear, both outside and inside church; for as an ex-Convener of the Kirk's Committee on Public Worship, he would no doubt have stringent tests to apply to much contemporary music before conceding its helpfulness to a christian spirituality. There has been, in these sixty years, a revolution: in attitudes to theology, in experience of religion, and in the practice of worship; and simultaneously an earthquake in the technology of music and entertainment. The time seemed ripe, therefore, to attempt an up-date on these earlier lectures. And it seemed appropriate to essay such an attempt in the heart of Glasgow during its Year of Culture. For three reasons, the least significant being that in that year the General Assembly met in Glasgow for the first time for centuries.

The other two reasons were related to culture in its wider sense. First, that the deepening concentration of the arts in Glasgow, in counterpoint to the more overtly 'cultured' Athens of the North (Edinburgh), reminded us that liturgy is not a hobby for musical or ministerial mandarins, but is the work of the people; and second, the location of the lectures, in an elegant hall - a regular venue for concerts - reminded us that the people of God live in a world, not a church. What they give worth to will resonate in their lives during the week more regularly than on Sundays. And what they bring to worship will reflect what is happening in the cultural arena where they spend their lives. In the course of these lectures, therefore, I cast the net more widely than my predecessor did, for the river of culture lands on the shore of each generation material that would be not only unfamiliar to earlier generations of worshippers, but alien. We, in our time, are not only talking about new kinds of musical instruments and new musical styles; not only talking about new ecclesiastical uses of dated musical styles - nothing dates so painfully as popular fashion - we are talking also about the worlds of film, video, theatre, rock and pop events, personal stereo, and non-stop radio, and we're talking about a world pervaded by television - which is where I came in. Those who can, do. Those who can't, lecture. I'm a worse case. I'm a musician whose shelf life ended a long time ago, so I cannot, in the full professional sense, do. As for lecturing, I never even aimed at that. However, I too, had my hour. For those who can't do, and don't usually lecture, there is always television.

Into broadcasting, therefore, I gravitated as naturally as a mollusc to its seabed, remaining there for over a quarter of a century.

I did come on to the beach for five years, as minister of the Old Parish Church of Peterhead, a few miles from its rival town of Fraserburgh where my father delivered that epilogue 30 years before. But even in that parish I remained active in ITV and BBC programmes. So in assessing what merit or otherwise lies in the views I now hold in respect of church music, at least it cannot be said that the changing trends of the quarter century have passed me by. I think I can say I have seen them all, participated in not a few, and initiated some. So what are my views?

Let me, in the first place, put it like this. I am unimpressed by trends - including, if it comes to that, any trend to resist trends. I am unimpressed by all rigid positions. But that is decidedly not a vote for modernism - in whatever trendy form - over against a rigid traditionalism. Oh no. For nothing, I repeat for the hard of inner hearing nothing, is so rigid as the latest trend. Look at it statistically. Add up all the trends of the last - let's be generous - five hundred years. Put that as one hundred points, twenty per century. The latest trends of the last twenty five years will summon up five points. A flexible approach will not say we must excommunicate 95% of the available material - because it is traditional - in order to accord to the 5% that is recent the special authority of an over-riding truth. This would not be charismatic vision. It would be merely tunnel vision - and a very wee tunnel.

I am not competing for a job, so I will not seek to amaze with the range of my *curriculum vitae*. It would fail to impress. Traditionalists would shake their heads at so many years wasted on the musical husks that the trendy swine had left, while serious trendies would shrug their shoulders at such painful failure to be truly radical. What I will do, therefore, is in line with what I have done throughout this personal survey of where we are in church music: I will reminisce. Here are some moments, mainly musical, but by no means exclusively so. Just as theatre and liturgy are historically intertwined, so in my life it was round an emotionally interchangeable array of theatres, auditoria and churches that my developing perspectives constellated.

I first had a literary interest in the theatre, sustained in my youth, for example, by delicious experiences in Edinburgh's Lyceum Theatre: a dark winter matinée with Dame Edith Evans decanting heady wine from the now untrendy verse drama of Christopher Fry's 'The Dark Is Light Enough'. Or in the same theatre a Festival evening when Jean Louis Barrault distilled a Danish prince from an Avon wordsmith via a French text of 'Hamlet'. But I had a musical interest, too. As a music student I played Bach on an off-stage harmonium, while a yawning actor of uncertain years let his hands wander uncertainly over the keys of an onstage harmonium during the most boring play ever written for or performed on a western stage. It boasted the title, 'It Is Midnight, Dr Schweitzer', and by the end of each evening's performance it felt like midnight, as not only was the audience, the cast, the producer, the catering staff and the theatre cat asleep, but also, one evening, my left knee - with the result that, lacking sufficient air from the bellows, the final Bach prelude fell prey to the terminal malaise which, according to the text of this prune of a play, was rife everywhere except the bamboo hut of the saintly doctor on the stage of the Church of Scotland's Gateway Theatre, Edinburgh.

The same year, a worse fate befell my right hand. Again offstage - was destiny already telling me something? - I was contracted, this time on a notably ungrand upright piano, to let Beethoven's 'Moonlight' and 'Appassionata' Sonatas thunder tinnily across the King's Theatre in Glasgow. The heroine played with moonlit passion at an on-stage grand. The play was the psycho-drama, 'The Seventh Veil', also a famous James Mason film. It all went like clockwork until the last performance on the Saturday night. The heroine hammered out the last chords, flung her hands dramatically into the air, and in a marked manner rose from the piano stool. My right hand slipped and extracted a meatily gratuitous chord from an apparently unattended piano. A ripple of Saturday night appreciation - to put it more plainly, gales of Glasgow laughter - ran round the theatre. What ran round the stage a few minutes later, was the red-haired actress. No cleaver being handy, I survived. But my life in showbusiness didn't.

It had all begun innocently enough when I was in my teens. I had taken part in operas staged in my school, that castellated essence of *château* which guards the humble citizens of Comely Bank from the Arctic gales that blow over from Fife. At Fettes, we had a music master the divine scale of whose musical goofiness was in inverse proportion to his height. His name was Tommy Evans. He bounced on the balls of twinkling feet, and smoked a pipe the density of whose effusions entirely removed his top half from sight. The *basso profundo* of utterances proceeding from this cloud on Sinai encapsulated more scholarly common-sense in an afternoon's lesson than one would get from a lifetime's study of The Oxford Companion To Music.

Lurking, however, in the fingertip finesse of this gentle man was a manic entrepreneur. He smiled through gaps in the smoke at the musical sixth one day and said, (puff, puff) "I am about to lay a rather large egg." (puff, puff) To the applause of the musical sixth, and the bewilderment of the rest of the school, he did. We gave a full-scale performance of Smetana's opera 'The Bartered Bride', using the English text by Edward Dent, the operatic editor and translator whom Tommy took me to meet in

Covent Garden. This "Bride" was real showbiz stuff. Smetana's circus rampaged through the audience - this is *de rigeur* nowadays, but was novel anywhere in the Forties, let alone in a public school devoted to rugby football. The following year, Tommy got us to do a full-scale performance of Weber's opera 'Der Freischutz'.

At the same time that the genius of my organ guru Bill Minay was lowering me into the worshipful depths of Bach, Tommy Evans was hoisting me on the hype of music as theatrical fun. Neither then nor since would worship and fun seem in my mind to be separate.

After school, my theatrical music-making ranged from the eclectic to the apoplectic. I provided a piano accompaniment to Ibsen's 'Peer Gynt' - loose Mackenzie bolted on to disembowelled Grieg; I sang the lead part in Britten's 'Let's Make An Opera', and I rolled with the punch-lines in 'Varsity Vanities'. I gave musical culture evenings to Mormons, compered hours of *soirées musicales* at student conferences, played cricket for the Faculty of Music in my pyjamas, and drinking songs for the Faculty of Divinity in my *lederhosen*. My introduction to broadcasting took an eccentric form. Moultrie Kelsall, a famous actor and radio producer who was to become even more famous as the aquiline presence brooding over porridge and coffee at the Laigh Café, was producing a radio documentary on Eric Liddell, thirty five years before 'Chariots of Fire'. I was commanded to deliver to the Queen Street Studios on a Sunday afternoon thirty or forty well-lunged men who would combine the roles of healthy Christian students singing a raucous farewell to Liddell at Waverley Station, and starving prisoners of war intoning a mournful hymn in a Far Eastern hell-hole.

It was I who was singing a mournful hymn as the witching hour of the recording approached, and almost none of the random rabble of Music, Divinity, and Arts faculty singers and rugger players I had jauntily invited had turned up. The memory of Moultrie Kelsall's expression as he faced an empty imaginary Waverley Station with a female assistant and a choirless conductor, lent to my subsequent negotiation of the

Laigh porridge experience a lumpy aspect. They did all turn up, a little late, but I fear Moultrie's production values were compromised by the rumbustious vocalising of those prisoners of war who were in somewhat virile form after what passed for pub lunches in those days, an undefined number of pints, accompanied by a possibly over-defined number of pies.

So it went on, from one oddity to another. All great fun, all grist to the mill... but... the fact of the matter was that underneath I was a rather serious guy, and all this fun was actually less fun than the other kind of theatre and music in my life which was serious stuff. That, you see, was taking place in the theatre of my mind. And what was going on there was words. Let me explain about words.

For me, one of the highlights of the BBC Scotland television series 'The Quest', was a conversation with Michael Redington, once my boss in ITV. He is a media man through and through. He transformed religious television in its early years by his visionary treatment of God on the box. His weapons were images and his basic strength lay in his intuition. For him, one felt, feeling was all. Yet in this televised conversation he said, "In the beginning was the Word, and in the theatre, words are everything. Everything follows from the words."

If the proof of the pudding is in the eating, Michael Redington has plum duff coming out of his ears. In recent years he has become a spectacularly successful impresario on the London West End stage. And how? By having a nose for a good script. '84 Charing Cross Road', 'Jeffrey Bernard Is Unwell', you name an unexpected off-beat idea which has taken off to critical acclaim and box office success, and Michael seems to have been its progenitor. Because he got the words right. The reason I never consummated, as it were, a career in music - apart from incidental factors such as possible limitations in the areas of talent and diligence - is that in the theatre of my mind I was divided between music and words, and words won.

It is somehow characteristic that here I am talking and writing about music. The battle was joined early and pursued down the years into adulthood; and I can tell you of the moment when it was all over. In the early Sixties, my wife and I were having a weekend break in a hotel in St. Ives in Cornwall. I went for a stroll in the grounds before turning in. A vast harvest moon eyed me over a hill. "Yes," I said to it, "yes, OK, yes, I agree, I've got to make this choice finally, don't I? It's absurd at my advanced age to have a split mind over my life's work. So, which is it to be?" The answer was obvious, so I went to my room and said to Elizabeth, "It's words." She knew what I meant and listened to my proviso - that I would try to incorporate into my use of words musical values, so that whatever I had picked up from the practice and observation of music would not have been wasted. I may have failed, but that is what I have tried to do, in the pulpit, in broadcasting, in writing, and in trying to work out what categories are useful in thinking about the universe we inhabit.

There were two reasons why this was an inevitable decision. The first is that, even when pursuing music as my apparent priority, I had always had a programme approach to it. For me there never was pure unprogrammed music. The composer might write a symphony. I turned it into a tone-poem. Even a fugue became a story in the theatre of my mind. I turned flesh into words.

The second reason was that I was genetically determined by generations of pulpit occupiers to occupy not just a theatre in my mind but a pulpit. Give me a subject and I would climb into a mental pulpit and preach on it. How tiresome! Well, actually, no. I found it rather fun. That was the serious fun I enjoyed. When I was eleven, two boys in Fraserburgh came round on a Saturday afternoon to ask me out to play. My father informed them that I was whiling away my Saturday playing the organ in the church. He told me later that they were aghast. How could I whittle away my childhood Saturday freedom by voluntarily practising voluntaries? But, you see, the church was huge fun. It was, in the first place, huge. It was empty. I could fill it with splashes of sound, fury, and, through the *voix céleste*, seduction. The whole word drama of a meaningfully evolving universe was being played out under my hands and feet. Churches were actually exciting. They were waiting for something to happen: for the *Logos* to turn up.

I said in Chapter Three that the essence of music is wider than music. I'm now saying that the Word is wider than words. I'm saying that the cosmos, the world, and every human life is a theatre for form, drama, and articulation; and that liturgy is the religious name for this. Shakespeare, of course, as usual said it first: "All the world's a stage". Trevor Nunn told an English colleague of mine how once near Stratford he engaged in casual conversation two old local men who were cutting hedges at the roadside. They demonstrated how it was done. One said, "Oi rough-hews 'em and 'e shapes their ends." Who was Will Shakespeare but a local Stratford lad who magicked, by his sense of the music in words, the experiences of his life into the universal theatre of the human mind? But most of our hewing is rough. I hope I have conveyed, in my stories about school and after, the sense of muddle, inadequacy, and sometimes bathos that attended my explorations into music.

It's seldom an easy ride. Mozarts and Simon Rattles do not grow on trees. Tommy Evans, launching operas into a then philistine school, suffered problems with discipline, and a massive breakdown. Hewing can be rough. Edwin Muir's scathing line about preachers, "The word made flesh, made word again", tells a true story about the tragedy of an image and music starved tradition; but it isn't the whole story. The procession of fine minds and sensitively crafted speech that has distinguished the Scottish pulpit down the centuries has given birth to many a human tune and turned many a life into a symphony. In Scottish church life, the preacher has struck gold in the mining of spiritual music more often than the musician. For the simple reason that the musician hasn't, in Scotland, been given the chance. There never was, for most Scots, a golden age of church music.

I would like to make, for my present purposes, an arbitrary distinction between the phrase 'The Age Of Gold', which is my heading for this chapter, and the idea of a 'Golden Age'. A golden age is a period you can (at least in theory) locate in history, barnacled though it may be with mythical values by now. The values attached to a golden age put it in such a glowing light that it attracts profound nostalgia. If only, echoing Milton, Shelley and Tennyson, we could return to the practices and values of that time, our fundamental problems would be solved. There are, of course, three obvious and fatal snags. The first is that we cannot return. The second is that, even if we could, we would find it wasn't so golden after all. The third is that even if it was, it wouldn't solve our problems now; for everything evolves. Our on-board computers have accumulated information, values, images, sounds, associations, and patterns unknown to our predecessors. These can't be unlearned or disinvented and, unknown to us, they have altered in even the most traditional of us our perceptions, our tastes, our emotional patterns of response; and the alteration is permanent. We cannot travel to the golden age. It has gone away.

The 'age of gold' on the other hand, or so I would like to suggest, is entirely mythical. It is suspended in an imagined past or future, and we view it at an infinite distance. Being mythical, it is, in the obvious sense, not there. But equally, it is not not there. Since it has never come, it has never gone. Nor will it go, so long as people with imaginations wish to travel there. The age of gold is, in its past manifestation, Paradise before it was lost. In its future form, it is Paradise Regained. Looking back, it is the unspoiled Garden of Eden. Looking forward, it is the Kingdom come. At the dawn of time it was heaven. When the golden sun sets over history, it will be the new heaven and the new earth.

As myths these are not half bad, moreover they are necessary. For in the brief span of our mortality we do not only inhabit the time between birth and death, but the gap between a dreamed of world of unspoiled value and the stained world of what is called reality. And of course, as those who have followed me thus far will not be surprised to hear me say, there is a hint of magic in the concept of an age of gold.

Magic is another word for what we want but have been persuaded by experience rationally not to expect. From Shakespeare's 'The Tempest' to Hollywood's 'E.T.', mythical worlds blandish us away from a sullen acceptance of the dull, the drab, the mediocre and the monotonous towards a hope that magic is not only a myth, that God's in His Heaven and one day all will be right with the world; and that the Age of Gold will come round again.

Is there a connection between the golden age, the actual past time that provokes nostalgia, where the golden oldies of childhood still bloom; and the mythical age of gold where everything was and will be perfect? The connection is in oneself. It is through the race memory flowing in each of us that history happens, that the past makes available to the future whatever our generation thinks has a value worth passing on. Which brings us to the crunch question: what, then, is worth passing on? The short answer is: The Truth. But how do we pass on the truth?

The first step in answering that is so obvious as to be banal. At least we must not act as contraceptives to prevent five centuries of musical material flowing through to regenerate the spirits of our successors. I hope we can agree on that without any preliminary disputation: pausing only to note that, by definition, that means that most of what we pass on will be traditional.

The difficult question is slightly different: what is it that we are to add to those five centuries?

I began to discern one possible answer on an autumn afternoon in 1962. It happened on the stage of the Lyceum Theatre in Edinburgh, where some years before I had drunk in Edith Evans' distillation of 'The Dark Is Light Enough'. I think I have indicated that I like theatres. I like theatres very much. Like an empty church, an empty theatre hangs on the senses like a branch heavy with unblown blossom.

On that 1962 afternoon, the theatre was empty. On the stage were myself and Donald Swann. He, sitting at the piano, myself, standing respectfully to starboard of the piano lid. I was responsible, with a hymn writer called Peter Cutts, for the music of a conference of the World Student Christian Federation to take place the following January. Practical questions were beginning to exercise me.

How was one to provide words and music for a thousand students in Bristol's Coulson Hall, which would cover a spectrum of national cultures, liturgical cults, ideological positions, and theological schools so broad that just about the only common factor would be the Movement's hymn-book, 'Cantate Domino', not a bad one for an ecumenical collection, but already somewhat dated?

I had read or heard that Donald Swann, having won his spurs as a brilliant light entertainer with Michael Flanders, was now composing religious music. Donald, a man of profound attentiveness to the needs and aspirations of others, invited me, a perfect stranger, to join him on the Lyceum Stage for a ruminative rummage through ideas before the evening show.

But being Swann, what he played and sang to me was not Swann, but Carter. It is difficult to believe now, but as short a time ago as 1962, Sydney Carter was unknown.

As Donald showed me this Carter song, then that, sang this one, played another, a dim awareness of a new voice crept up the nape of my neck and broke into my ear the phial of a singular new reality. It was a curious setting for a new world to break into one's consciousness: an empty stage; a baby grand; a smiling musician's head bobbing and weaving, his hands caressing and carousing, his light tenor addressing itself to the unbearable lightness of being Sydney Carter; and a young Scottish male Christian's eyes widening as at a new landscape seen from a mountain pass. The hundreds of empty red seats in that exquisite old theatre soon stopped yawning and lapsed into an appreciative hush. Thus I first heard 'The Lord of the Dance', 'It was on a Friday Morning', and other songs which Sydney had just composed.

Thus I learned, if I needed to learn, that the way forward for religious song is neither by defending traditional music, nor by attacking it; is neither by campaigning for new fashions in church music, nor by resisting them; is neither by abandoning old techniques and instruments nor excluding new ones; but the way forward is by having something to say and something to listen to. In the context of The Way, The Truth and The Life, it is not a way forward that we want, any more than a way back, but a way that is true to life at a given time and place. Music which lives by the guitar will perish by the guitar, but the same is true of the pipe organ, the Yamaha, the clapping choir and the clarsach. All these are the clothes worn or not worn by the Emperor of Truth. Divine truth may have its origin in the stars, but it has its roots in human lives and it seeks lodging in common minds.

When you hear a song by Sydney Carter, either played and sung with the accomplished zest of Donald Swann or rasped out by Sydney himself, what you are having access to is a man being himself, and sharing that with you. Put like that, it sounds a modest, not to say banal achievement. But actually most of us are not at all skilled at sharing what we are. Even with friends it is far from easy to communicate the essence of what we are about. To find a form in which to convey that to strangers without, along the way, losing the raw authenticity of unvarnished truth, why, if we could all do that we'd have honest politics, unstressed businessmen, unburned-out clergy, no divorce, no accidental wars, and a very boring life for the police. In other words, Utopia, the Age of Gold, would have arrived.

Nevertheless, we should try, and Sydney is one who in our time has given us pointers.

In January 1963, Bristol had its worst blizzard in living memory. Despite traffic grinding to a stop for days, the thousand students arrived, and eclectic really is the only suitable word for the musical diet we offered. Golden Oldies vied with Nasty Newcomers, but most of it was a tasteful and robust enough selection from trad and modern. For the climactic worship I devised a nice little liturgical nightmare. As an exercise in topicality, we invited the conference to listen to Top Of The Pops on the BBC on the Friday evening, and, having thus ascertained what was number one, to write words for it which we would have as the key hymn on the Saturday. The top disc was duly revealed to be 'Telstar' by The Shadows, and out of scores of submissions, we selected a Resurrection lyric which, rehearsed and delivered by a thousand voices, made a more than audible peroration to the week.

Carter songs figured in that January of 1963, but the unravelling of what had come alive on the Lyceum stage with Donald Swann took place over many years.

In the summer of 1964, I was responsible for arranging a study conference of the Student Christian Movement at Swanwick, on the theme of science. I worked on this with the physicist Claude Curling, a synthesiser of scientific and theological images partly along the lines of Teilhard de Chardin, but with sharp insights of his own. I had met Claude on Iona when I was organising the music there and Claude had been brought to the island by Ralph Morton, the Deputy Leader, to give summer lectures on the ethics and theology of nuclear power. Claude's approach to scientific reality was liturgical, in the wide sense in which I have been using that word. Like George MacLeod, but with more technical collateral, he saw coherent movement and harmony in the micro-sub-atomic world, and in the macro world of the cosmos. He did not only see in his research, but felt in his bones, the dance of the stars from whose atomic furnace all the dances of life flow. So we made this science conference liturgical.

Swanwick, the hallowed conference venue for generations of students and church leaders, where I first heard Shirley Williams on the ethics of politics, and Erik Routley on the ethics of music, was transformed that burning July of 1964 into a liturgical force field. Instead of talks, lectures, study groups, sub-groups and seminars, we had language laboratories, cybernetic experiments, astronomic apparatus, and liturgical, artistic, and musical workshops. Sydney Carter led evening scientific processions from the main buildings to the chapel, when he wove together in pungent unaccompanied song the themes and discoveries of the day. One group had to calculate exactly when the first Russian sputnik would cross the Swanwick lawn. At some early hour beyond midnight, the conference danced, with Sydney in attendance, on the lawn, as that early icon of the human liturgy invading space obligingly passed overhead.

In the following year, I found myself producing religious programmes on the ITV network. My closest colleague was Ben Churchill, a brilliant Light Entertainment producer with a subtle grasp of the rhythms of both the human mind and the numinous. He produced a stunningly simple series of music programmes called 'Hallelujah'. Looking back, I marvel at how good they were. Sydney Carter linked them and sang. Nadia Cattouse also sang, and the backing was exquisitely sensitive. I recall flute playing out of this world. Now, what kind of music was this? It was religious, for in the links Sydney probed with his Socratic tongue the aching nerve of many a theological tooth, and the figure of Jesus was seldom far away. But this all happened in sessions in the studio. It had nothing to do with the church as such. Most of the songs were on the level of human experience rather than divine interpretation; and dilemmas were not always resolved with Christian vocabulary. Indeed, dilemmas were not always resolved.

The programmes were, I would aver, truthful. The words and music stated fairly, I think, what Karl Barth called "the state of affairs", and so I feel free to draw over that little group the protective shield of theological approach that Karl Barth draws over Wolfgang Amadeus Mozart; that he is the pagan *par excellence*, the creature who accepts his role in creation and does not compete through an egocentric and ersatz spirituality with the divine. But there are two other points to be made. First, Sydney's links really were truthful - to the extent of being uncomfortable - as a result of which there were periodic skirmishes with the controlling authority at the IBA. The lesson from that is: the first contribution the pulpit can make to the progress - or survival - of a meaningful church music is truth from the pulpit, however much it hurts. Second, Ben Churchill had a production technique which almost never failed. He had recording equipment on standby, but never used it until... until what? Until the moment came. What moment? Just the moment. He would get the performers to chat, sing, play, have coffee, relax, concentrate a little, pause, try another song - and then quite suddenly, hey presto, he sensed the soufflé was about to rise, and the programme was recorded. The lesson for church music is not that the congregation can be asked to wait till the choir is suddenly in the mood, or the choir and organist wait till tongues of flame settle on the congregation, but that quality of performance does depend on atmosphere and that timing is of the essence.

I have seen more services go wrong through a jangling atmosphere and clumsy timing than by poor technical accomplishment. In fact in the late 1960s, I produced a huge Christmas Eve bonanza from Liverpool Cathedral, with the Bee Gees, The Settlers, Kenny Everett, and a thousand teenagers dancing, which was ruined because at the very last moment the Dean, Edward Patey, who had been brave enough to let all this happen, lost his nerve. Just before the recording, he stepped to the mike and said, "Don't forget, this is a cathedral." In a split second, the atmosphere died. The programme, which would have been magic, was merely busy.

Five years later, in Peterhead, a lively BBC programme from the Muckle Kirk with music by Peterhead Academy was almost destroyed when the then school rector suddenly snapped and told two of the jazz band to get their hair cut. The band went on strike. Only the intervention of the music master, Tom Galloway, accepted by both sides as an honest broker, saved the day.

There are three immensely important positive lessons here. First, seriously consider letting in cultural forces from outside the church, whoever they are. Don't limit yourself to the churchy versions of them, which may be pale reflections. Second, once you've asked them in, trust them totally. You must allow them to be themselves, or they won't come back. Why should they? Third, don't think you're doing them a favour. Realise their material may be where authentic truth lies. Good serious jazz is nearer Bach than almost anything else I know. Wasn't Bach sacked by a kirk session for improvising too wildly?

This is not a discourse on music on television, so I will pass over other musical experiments we engaged in, coming to a climactic series near the end of my time in ITV which we called, 'Don't Just Sit There'. The musical *genii* we let out of the lamp included Sydney Carter, Donald Swann and Erik Routley. There was a studio audience, and a lot of participation. It was lively, but also practical. The principal point being made was, as the title suggests, that church music is not a process in which the people in the pew are passive victims of what experts visit upon them.

The river of religious television has flowed on since those days of the late '60s, but I am not sure that it has flowed outwards to a great sea of enhanced consciousness. Rather, I fear the reverse.

For all its faults, the era of the '60s was a time of exploration. Now, at least in broadcasting, religious music has drawn in its horns. I have not been a feverish admirer of 'Songs of Praise' and 'Highway'. I respect the strong service to mainstream Christianity of 'Songs of Praise'. Skilful producers work long hours to enable fine performers of hymn classics and new songs and hymns to sweep over Britain on Sunday evenings. The filmed interviews which punctuate and motivate the hymns are sometimes little masterpieces of their kind. But what is their kind? Heavily edited cameos of faith, typically describing a role in the community whose worthiness justifies choosing the subject of interviewing; and recounting an experience, frequently of suffering, which has confirmed the person's faith. The second last question put to the interviewee is "What hymn have you chosen?" The final question is "Why?" The answer to this is not always illuminating, and sometimes the interviewer has the sense to dispense with a device which can amount to little more than a blatantly artificial link into the next hymn. Radio Scotland's senior radio producer, Johnston McKay did this better when in the series, 'It Strikes A Chord', listeners from all over Scotland were allowed to speak at uninterrupted length about their favourite hymn, with results in which the homely mingled with the profound.

On the Sunday evening 'Win A Ratings War For God' slot
- the ITV series 'Highway' was in some ways worse, and in other
ways better, than 'Songs of Praise'. The ways in which it was
worse are not difficult to determine. The production values of
the BBC series have the integrity of time and space, of committed communities, and of music of a professional standard.
'Highway's' sense of place was as rooted as a piece of soap in the
bath, but not even the most perfumed soap is accompanied by
a mellifluous ensemble so ubiquitous that its signature tune
should be 'I'll Walk Beside You'. As Harry Secombe strolls over
a grassy knoll, a ruined abbey, a city square, or a village green,
there glides beside him, just out of camera range, an unseen
orchestra. In fact, of course, it is there in neither time nor place,
but recorded in studio. The Secombe script, as it lurches into
verbal engagement with a characterful person of the region,
might be said to be long on brevity, short on wit, ambivalent on
factuality - but big on warmth.

And that warmth is important. While watching 'Highway'
(yes, I did watch it) I sometimes thought: this is actually rather
good. Note the actually. Theoretically, it is awful. Musically,
patchy. Intellectually, feeble. Televisually, primitive. But actually, I would realise, this is touching me where it matters - in the
heart. Secombe is a genuine man, and he brings out the genuine
in others. His walks across greensward may be stagey, but his
singing is full bodied. Above all, the very vulgarity of the format
sometimes let in a humanity, which in its awful and funny
reality could be a very vulgar and warm thing.

I don't think we get anywhere by dismissing any form of
religious music making. After all, if a minister and Kirk Session
were offered free Harry Secombe, the backing orchestra, an
additional soloist and a chorus or two, would it not seem
sensible to jump at the opportunity? Ah, but that is precisely
the point. Normal congregations do not have that offer made
to them. So what are they to do? Shrink before the relentless
onslaught of showbiz religion on the telly (and it will increase,
as proliferating channel outlets allow in more and more evangelical hard sells)? Grovel in front of the ceaseless movement of

style and mood in the mass commercial music market, as that hits and envelopes the younger end of the market? Should the local congregation, totally unable to compete, just apologise for existing, or go the whole hog, give up entirely, and shut up shop?

No, pressing the panic buttons is not the way to find truth in a life situation; and for Christians after all, it is not a matter of a way forward or a way back, but a way: a truthful way, that we seek.

It is about time to wave goodbye to 'Songs of Praise' and 'Highway', and the other programmes they spawn such as Thora Hird being absolutely astonished to see you as she sits in her parlour and fishes in her handbag for the letter you sent her; or Roy Castle exploring the history of European castles and coming up, my goodness, with Taizé monks humming Gelineau; but before we leave all that apparently successful hymnological juggernauting, let's ask: why do people watch these programmes, and in sufficiently large numbers to justify ratings - chasing television tycoons leaving them there at prime time?*

It's very simple. They are hole in the heart operations. People have a hole in their hearts, and they seek something, anything, which will alchemise that gap into a wholeness. So they look for someone they can identify with and if they feel they can trust that person, they may open up enough to receive a piece of music - in the wide sense I've been using - a piece of intuition, a revelation, a tune of the mind. All that is asked of the actual sound patterns is that they should midwife that inner music into their minds. Harry Secombe and Thora Hird, perpetually cheery though they are on camera, also have the kind of crushed pineapple faces that suggest that they have suffered, felt emotions, had to work a bit at living. Their faces look lived in. But the other trick is the faces of the members of the public who sing. The genius of 'Songs of Praise' is the lived

---

* The new ITV tycoons did remove 'Highway' from prime time in January 1993. 'Songs of Praise' remains, but only after internal argument. Jonathan Powell, Controller BBC1 until December 1992, wanted to move 'Songs of Praise' back to tea-time, but was over-ruled.

in look of the faces that tell their story, not only in interviews, but as you read their eyes in the singing of words that connect with their life experience. Now all these commodities, the ones that animate and sell the programmes, are not only available in the local church, they are the genius of the average church congregation, the stuff it is made of, they are why it exists and what it does and what it does best: namely, being human, suffering, working at being alive, getting through. All that is required is what I identified as the source of Sydney Carter's distinctive authority: being himself and sharing that self with others. What is asked of each congregation - and this is a *sine qua non* of a serious recovery of magic in church music - is a minister or priest who acts and speaks truthfully, a leader of the music who is vulnerable in his or her basic relationships, which means listening a great deal to others, and worshippers who are motivated to share the raw grit of their lives. By that I don't mean a sharing which has to be explicit, but an attitude of openness. These qualities in themselves will not produce musical solutions, but without them, musical dilemmas are unlikely to be solved.

Is that all? Do we abandon the entire project of ratiocination, the ladder built rung by rung from inarticulate cavemen, from level to level of civilisation, culture, artistic construction, and the philosophical, scientific, and theological struggle to apprehend and formulate, just to sit in a pew with our minds, emotions, and mouths wide open, like baby birds in a nest? But that would not be being open at all. That would be to act a childish part, and I fear that if the mood of some charismatic and evangelical worship is of a temper I cannot identify with, it is precisely because of the implicit or explicit demand to empty one's brain and submit. All I have been saying is directed at the opposite pole: the necessity not to be passive victims of a worship juggernaut, but to be active, at least in the imagination. The essence of being open is to be yourself, and that means to be fully yourself, with sensuality, logic, imagination, and spirit all available. This is where we return to the struggle between word and music which faced me in my own life; to the principle which a successful showbiz impresario brings to his theatre work, that "in the beginning is the word", and we return to the basis of the liturgy of the Church of Scotland, which is word and sacrament: the word first, then the active physical forms of response.

To clinch that point, I am going to share with you moments that conveyed sacramental truth to me. Most of them occurred in the fairly showbizzy setting of television, but you will note that the essence of what happened had little or nothing to do with surface glamour, glitzy expertise, or exhibitionist performance. They were moments of truth because in each case human beings were vulnerable in the active communication of word and music, and I call that sacramental.

During our filming of a pub in Shettleston Road, Glasgow, one Friday evening, a Salvation Army lady officer came in collecting. We didn't expect her. She didn't expect us. Some men, fairly well advanced in the evening's business of getting inside a jar, insisted that she sang. They went further. They specified what she was to sing. And so, in an environment as alien as could be imagined to the proper experience of worship, she embarked on 'The Old Rugged Cross'. There was, both that evening, and when Paul Streather, the director, came to edit, one problem: the woman couldn't sing. The pub aficionados were beyond caring, but the film editor, a man of conscience, cared strenuously. He objected to our putting on the air this musically excruciating, utterly out of tune, parody of a much loved hymn, which was publicly to humiliate the woman. Paul consulted me, and we finally came to an agreement: her sincerity was so clear and the listening faces around in the pub so marked by rugged experience that the discordant nature of the melodic line made the old words ring out as new. Not only had Paul the wit and courage to hold the shot throughout the singing, but he had the courage not to edit it down. I can still feel myself in that cutting room, in that pub, in my own life when events tangle and snarl and hurt, hearing that sacramental breaking of a voice. This was liturgy. This was authentic church music. And all it took was one brave woman being true to her belief, unapologetic about an emotional religious song, and willing to take a risk and to go over the top. No, there was one other factor: a congregation vulnerable enough to share the moment with her; for, though there may have been an element of gentle teasing when they twisted her arm to sing, by the end the men were moved.

Tongue, in Sutherland, is as far from Shettleston Road as you can get in mainland Scotland: if you ever have the chance, go there. It must be among the dozen most beautiful places in the world. I had better qualify that. It is uniquely beautiful or conspicuously lacking in beauty, depending on what is beautiful for you. It is a Highland village, but when you've said that you've said nothing. It is the mane of a neck of land between the waters of the Kyle of Tongue and an upheaval of ground known, inadequately, as Ben Loyal. "Loyal", as the infatuated minister, Alfie McLintock called her, is a very weird mountain. I will say no more, for Ben Loyal's brooding stance makes me nervous. Anyway, we went there to film and record the congregation singing psalms and hymns. Half the people were Gaelic speakers. Most had Gaelic ancestry. Their faces were profound. Their singing was raw. When they rose to sing a psalm, a wind from beyond Time soughed through the trees.

I had to stop our Music Adviser rehearsing them, for he could not resist trying to 'improve' their performance. Improve it? They were already in touch with the ultimate, and expressing it. How do you improve on that? The sad *dénouement* is this. When the programme was transmitted, the Tongue congregation felt humiliated. They had never before realised how bad they were. Television had destroyed their innocence. I feel contrite about that. 'Songs of Praise' you see, had become their standard. But, being translated, what had really happened is that 'Songs of Praise' had become their standardisation. That is diabolical. Just as some people, conceivably, may find the brooding shadows of Sutherland in general, and Tongue in particular, to be lacking in those chocolate box qualities that for Tourist Board brochure artists define scenic prettiness, so some people might, conceivably, have found the Tongue gouging out of psalms to be deficient in that brisk and cheerful choral polish which is the mark of 'Songs of Praise'. In which case, phooey to choral polish.

As far as you can get emotionally from Tongue in mainland Scotland is Troon, an exceedingly trim, well-behaved and well-behoofed municipality on the coast of Ayrshire. It has two distinctions of theatrical dimensions. It faces the mountains of Arran; and from time to time it hosts the Open Golf Championship. To describe it as genteel would be to give way to stereotypes. Let us rather describe it as discreet. Neither the rugged terrain of Sutherland mountains nor the rugged terrain of Shettleston faces disturb its orderly place in the scheme of things. When the Open is not on, the most exciting thing to happen is when, every couple of days, a plane lands at nearby Prestwick. You would not expect, therefore, a volcano of excitement when we recorded in Troon's Town Hall an aggregation of local choirs for a Scottish alternative to 'Songs of Praise'. But I will tell you of two exalting moments in these recordings. There was nothing visually exciting about the Hall; and the choirs were stood in conventional order at one end. What raised the emotional temperature to boiling point, and beyond that into a sort of mystical steam was the identity of the two people in charge of the recording. The first was Jim Clarke. Jim was Music Adviser to Ayrshire schools. I first heard him operate for a Scottish 'Songs of Praise' called 'Scotspraise', when he conducted local school choirs and instrumentalists. He did three things which impressed me enough to ask him to become Music Adviser to our Scottish hymn programmes. First, he phrased the melodic line with a courteous elegance which allowed the music to breathe, to ebb and flow, to achieve natural climaxes. He released the inner rhythm of a tune. Second, his speeds were geared to letting the words speak out truthfully, and this meant that many hymns were taken slower than most conductors would take them; and thirdly, he wrote super descants. The other person was May, a local Ayrshire girl who had become a director-producer of talent and courage, and put truth before surface impression.

Two moments still speak to me. In the hymn 'O Love That Wilt Not Let Me Go', May Bowie fastened a camera on an elderly lady and held that close shot for a whole verse. That takes directorial courage. It was worth it. That one face said absolutely everything. The other moment occurred in 'Abide With Me'. Jim wrote a descant which climbed to a sublime apex. And May, in one panning movement, matched the shot exactly to that apex. May, not a trained musician, decoded Jim's musical concept. Jim, an experienced musician, paid tribute to May as a director unusually sensitive to what he was trying to achieve. There are three lessons here. First, because the two operatives co-operated in mutual respect - they listened to each other - everything worked. Minister and musician must equally listen and co-operate. Second, two old chestnuts of hymns were dispatched into orbit because professionals were not too cautious or cynical to go over the top in their service. Third, commitment and passion can make the ordinary extraordinary. An old lady's face was for a whole minute the entire landscape of the Gospel; a bare municipal hall was alchemised into the Sistine chapel by a local choir, a local youth brass band, and a descant; and this all happened because a local conductor and a local television director went over the top with musical and televisual courage, to allow emotional phrasing of a majestically slow pace. The result might have been pretentiously heavy-handed. It was incandescent. The resources were modest. The ambition was Herculean, namely to tell the emotional truth, with no holds barred.

A long way south of Troon is Coventry. For the ITV God slot on New Year Sunday, 1967, we went to Coventry Cathedral. We didn't go there on a whim. Basil Spence's new cathedral was raised from the wreck of the medieval one burned out by fire on the night of the devastating German blitz of the 14th November 1940.

The new cathedral was built in reconciliation. That word has become flaccid through pious over-use. The reality is that creation is always New Creation - that is what the word means

- and creation transcends barriers not only the obvious ones of war and death, but also of time, fashion, and perception. Old and new are burned together in the crucible of what it is to be fully human. That is the ultimate sacrament.

But our programme for New Year 1967 began with the Word. The IBA Panel said the script was too left wing. Paul Tortelier kept telling me on the phone from Paris that it wasn't radical enough, that if we didn't tell the whole truth about the Vietnam War, we would insult those who died in Coventry. We eventually ignored the IBA and put it out. The IBA was very cross indeed, except the Scottish member, a quiet ex-Moderator called Tom Murchison. He was a Gaelic speaking man and he retrospectively defended us. "We Highlanders," he ruminated, "know about oppression and exploitation. We even know about being burned."

It was Human Rights Year and our cheerful atheist ex-boxer script-writer Trevor Preston - subsequently one of Britain's regular award-winning drama writers - wrote a radical script.

On the night the cast assembled: cellist Tortelier, guitarist John Williams, poet Adrian Mitchell, pianist Nerine Barrett, and singer Carolyn Hester. Two massive snags developed: the power supply failed; and Carolyn failed to arrive. The blizzard which affected the power had delayed the American plane. The director was another woman of courage, Helen Standage. She was small, but determined. She kept everyone motivated. In the early hours, we were still recording, snow falling on people's heads in the roofless ruin, and the lights still blazing in the new Cathedral. The recording ended at 2 am. Was all that glamorous? No, it was grim. But everyone was motivated. They believed in the word being spoken, so they let the word become flesh in them. To see and hear Tortelier saw away at his cello at one in the morning, his face yellow with fatigue, was to see God and hear what I would call music. What he was playing was unaccompanied Bach. Back to the past? Forward to the future? I don't know or care. It was the way at that moment. It was the Truth. It was Life. At such a moment, the Age of Gold is no myth. It is young again, and so are we.

In 1966 it became known at almost no notice that Duke Ellington was to play an evening of jazz in Coventry Cathedral with his own band, and to climax it with his religious cantata 'In The Beginning, God'. The ABC television management I was working under was led on its programme side by Controller Brian Tesler, later M.D. at LWT, and he said, "Get in there." Ben Churchill, the producer who was so skillful with the Sydney Carter programmes, got in there double quick and shot the evening without rehearsal. Only television professionals will fully understand how cheeky it was to shoot a major musical event entirely on the hoof. When you're dealing with jazz, the essence of which is to be unpredictable, the task is eerie. At the climax of the jazz peroration in the cantata - where the Creed says Jesus was crucified and rose from the dead - Ellington went into a kind of pianistic hyperventilation. At this point, Ben did an extraordinary thing. On the spur of the moment, he shut off all picture: the screen went black for a number of seconds which seemed like an eternity. This wasn't a failure of inspiration: it was sheer inspiration. It broke televisual rules: you simply aren't allowed to do that. So Ben did it. You see: you aren't really allowed to rise from the dead. It's against the rules.

So long as there are men and women like those I have mentioned in the media game, then it is not a trivial pursuit, but a way. These values, these challenges, these resurrections transcend our map of time. There is no old fashioned, or new fashioned: just, in every age, the tearing sound of costly truth being fashioned, the word becoming flesh; and that, I think the New Testament tells us, is the kind of music God is inclined to hear.

Chapter Six

MINING FOR GOLD

What is Truth? "Beauty is truth, truth beauty," wrote Keats, "that is all ye know on earth, and all ye need to know", thus ensuring that if his poetry failed to sell, at least he was assured a posthumous entry in a preacher's dictionary of quotations. As an impressionistic cry from the heart, it communicates. But as a proposition, it invites the retort: how do you know that is all you need to know? One person's beauty is another person's ugh! - so is one person's truth another person's lie? History is curiously unfair in its judgements on these matters. Socrates has had a favourable write-up for going round unsettling the young people of his day by asking them, "What is truth?", and submitting their answers to so many supplementaries that they became confused. Socrates is even more highly commended for the fact that in order to make the streets of Athens safe from confusion, he was dispatched to another dimension: where, presumably, he began at once to spread further confusion by asking, "What makes you think this is Heaven? How can we know what is heavenly?" Yet Pontius Pilate gets a bad press because he asked the same question. '"What is Truth?", asked Pilate, and did not wait for an answer' - that is how Bacon begins a famous essay. Pilate could have waited all day and not got an answer. This prisoner wasn't in the business of giving that kind of answer. What was Pilate supposed to have said? "Ah, Sir, I see from your silence that Truth is E equals MC^2, or alternatively, that truth is contained in the 'Sanctus' of the 'Mass in B Minor' which J.S. Bach will compose in about seventeen centuries from now?" Pilate's problem was, of course, that he asked a very good question at a very bad moment.

Pilate's unpopularity derives not from a dubious contribution to the footnotes of philosophy, but from his behaviour in a real life situation. In front of millions of angry putative readers of the New Testament, the poor guy washed his hands and let Barabbas get away, (that way, however, at least ensuring a posthumous entry in Bach's 'St. Matthew Passion'). But this leads us to a pivotal question. Can real truth be disentangled from real life? Is there such a thing as objective truth? My answer to that is put in one sense very simply: no. But that is my subjective answer. There is simply no way out of this ambiguity. It is a no-win situation. However, the person who, like Socrates, Pilate, or Alice in Wonderland, concedes that a definitive answer to the subjective/objective riddle may be difficult to come by, may be one half step ahead, through not obscuring the reality by formulae, however magisterial. Such a person (whether Socrates, Pilate, or Alice) recognises a fundamental ambiguity in all human language. Music, as one form of human language, is susceptible to that ambiguity.

In the second chapter, I described a recent visit to Prague. On one evening journey to a suburb we passed an Orwellian landscape of mass urban housing which I would describe in terms of tower blocks, except that that would be to put too kindly a construction on the architecture, as if these massive grey slabs were sufficiently individualistic and sky-orientated to deserve the word 'tower'. Michael Dean, the director of the film we were making, remarked that he had been considering the link between the Puritan ethic of self-denial and the Marxist totalitarian philosophy of denying self. In both cases, certain standards on a narrow front are preserved, but at the expense of freedom. It is now a truism of reportage by journalists and tourists alike that Eastern Europe has found freedom to deliver pornography, sleaze, and crime in sad proportion to deliverance from the knock on the door in the early hours. The challenge of choice which the cosmos delivers to us is not to be denied, a freedom where joy, colour, and wholeness are experimentally available, even if also available are the dark fruits of freedom. If you deny self, you deny that cosmos inside yourself which includes a range of opportunities in a lifetime to be wrong as well as right, to explore the dark as well as the light, evil as well as good, to go digging for real gold. If you deny that, you deny that for which we were born, which is creativity. And that includes the freedom to discover through play, like children, the possibilities of any medium. A bridge, or for that matter a tower block, must have flexibility built into it to take account of wind and variations in temperature: the structure must not be rigid. So any system constructed by the human brain, whether of theology, politics, morality, science, or art, if it is conceived rigidly or maintained and defended rigidly, will fail to keep up with real life as it is experienced by the human psyche, and will sooner or later break up under the strain.

A so-called objective approach to music will eventually fail. And so will a so-called objective approach to God. If you compound these failures by combining them in an objective approach to church music, you will not connect with reality as it is experienced by the mass of people for whom church music is meant to mean something. Which will enable them to face Monday morning.

But if I am trying to face reality, then I have to face one theological mountain that stands in the way. Or perhaps it is more a tower block, one that might be conceived by the science fiction writer Arthur C. Clarke, a tower stretching skywards so high you can't see the top, because it stretches beyond the earth's atmosphere, beyond the solar system, beyond the galaxy, beyond the Big Bang, to God Himself. Such a gargantuan structure might serve as a metaphor for the kind of theology which postulates an objective truth about God revealed from infinitely far away. It is what one could call a Jack in the Beanstalk theology, except that, whether it is tower block or beanstalk, it is built from the other end. As in Alice in Wonderland, where everything is upside down, so it is the top of this structure that hits the earth. This is of academic interest, since, whichever way the structure is built, its size is likely at some point to block out the light of experience. The rigidity of its structure, while it may provide adequate protection from some of the slings and arrows of outrageous fortune, is liable to fare less well when assailed by the massive earthquakes of emotional experience. According to some reports, if you visualise the structure as a tower block, the lift is working. Jacob confirms that angels were seen going up and down; but according to other stories, the giant gets restive from time to time and gives the whole thing a biff - there was an unfortunate incident at Babel - a misunderstanding over a language block. But the latest from the New Testament is that the giant in the beanstalk has been friendly for two thousand years, and the son of Jack is on remarkedly good terms with him.

In Scotland, revelation theology is represented at its most distinguished by Professor Tom Torrance. Also, at its most robust. He is not slow to reproach those who fail to see that this is how things are. In an article quoting the Life and Work of September 1990, The Glasgow Herald, under the banner headline, "Kirk beliefs attacked by Former Moderator", began its report by referring to a "scathing attack on attitudes in the Church of Scotland". One Torrance passage reads, "Obsession for relevance has led to a detachment of Christianity from Christ, and its attachment to society, so that the Christian way of life is re-interpreted to make it endorse the cheap humanistic philosophies of life placarded before our eyes by film and television. Christianity is reduced to being not much more than the sentimental religious froth of a popular socialism - the 'cheese and cookies notion of Christianity'. What Americans call 'car bumper theologies' replace the distinctive doctrines of the Christian faith, and trendy substitute religions replace strong evangelical witness to Jesus Christ as Lord and Saviour."

This is the gauntlet of 'objective' theology thrown down with gusto. Let us pick it up, for the phrase 'sentimental religious froth' will do very well as a pejorative label for a subjective approach to church music; while the dismissive wave of the hand towards film and television illustrates the failure of an 'objective' vision to see something in front of your eyes, in this case a common contemporary culture. I am not personalising this kind of theology in Tom Torrance to diminish him. One might as well seek to diminish the Sphinx by writing graffiti on it. But human thoughts and artefacts come down to stories, and stories are about people. The journey and struggle of faith is not on a separate plane. That is why so much of this series of lectures is stories about people.

In the '50s, I sat under Professor Torrance for three years. I was enchanted, as most of my fellow students were, by his personal warmth, his evangelical passion, and his lyrical use of language. Even, however, as I submitted emotionally to the appeal of the Torrance rhetoric, I gradually realised that what I was enjoying submitting to was not a series of objective statements, but a torrentially adjectival vision, with a cosmic Christ at the centre. The Torrance Dogmatics Lecture Sequence amounted to an epic love-poem, with Christ as the Beloved. This was, without reservation, a wonderful trip. The trouble arose when the poet launched into what he conceived as dialogue. He would lean over the lectern and elicit questions. He would answer them patiently and lovingly - so long as they were couched in what he regarded as appropriate language. If anyone, occasionally a bold Scot, but more frequently a sceptical American or German Ph.D. student, developed a challenge into a head-on assault on the divinity of Christ, the sun slid behind the cloud, and thunder rumbled. On one occasion, I recall a theological thunderbolt bouncing up the desks and striking a German who persisted in quoting with high voltage enthusiasm the arch-apostate (as Torrance saw him) German theologian, Rudolph Bultmann. For Bultmann, the question of whether Jesus actually rose from the dead or not is a secondary matter which distracts from the primary questions about whether in Jesus God came to us in the first place. Torrance, with a quiet conviction that chilled the blood, said, "You speak as the anti-Christ." At the coffee break, a once again sunny Torrance enquired of me, "I was right, wasn't I?" I wish I could recall my response.

He exhibited another trait which I have found to be not infrequent among evangelicals. They do not welcome arguments *ad hominem* applied to them, but they are capable of being *ad hominem* about you. At one lecture, just after College morning worship at which I had played the organ, Torrance singled me out of a class of thirty and addressed me on the subject of my organ voluntary. I was there and then the subject of an *al fresco* music review, delivered with crisp rhetorical elegance. At one level this was intellectually serious, educationally clever, pastorally sensitive, and personally flattering. Yet, I recognised even as I listened that as a music review this was flawed. I had played Bach. Was the piece I had played aesthetically defective? He didn't say. He was not at that point overtly concerned about music in worship nor about music itself. His concern was to use me and to use Bach, to make a point. The point was about Platonic idealism. As against the world-affirming Word made Fleshness of the Incarnate God in Christ (itself a concept I felt to be highly abstract) Bach, according to Torrance, had spiritualised religion into an ideal realm of abstract ideas.

At first I was impressed, but as the linguistic web was woven around me, I began to resile: on three counts. First, it seemed to me that what Professor Torrance attributed to Bach was a fair description of his own method; was the Torrance *corpus* of ideas not a gigantic abstract system clothed in the verbal equivalent of Bach melody and counterpoint? If so, Torrance was on his own terms, in action, a Platonist of a high order. Second, he was not really introducing a dialogue about Bach as a Platonist, he was painting a picture, valid in its own terms, which did not reflect my experience of Bach. Third, he was not submitting Bach's actual music to the rigorous analysis he would confer on a Biblical or Patristic text. I do not, of course, mean that Torrance was consciously doublethinking - any more than any of us do - but that at the centre of what was actually going on was a disjunction between claim and actuality. His image of his craft was that his language was objective and scientific. The actuality as I received it and responded to it was that it was a labyrinthinely poetic language, and indeed, now and then an almost Byronically romantic one. His own image of his teaching method was that he was humbly emptying his mind and heart before the revealed reality of God, receiving into the resultant space the Word of God, and sharing this treasure with us in a situation of dialogue. The actuality seemed to be that he was unveiling an *ex cathedra* revelation as to how we should think, see, hear, and feel.

I have gone into some detail about Professor Torrance and Bach for a number of reasons, of which one very practical one is this. At a less exalted level, many clergy still treat the musical element in worship and the organist in the vestry in an analogous way. A not untypical clergyman, (who knows little about music), assumes that he has more locus in the matter of music than the musician, (who knows little about theology), has in the matter of theology. When this is done with Torrance's brilliance and passion, it may be revelatory or obfuscating, but it is not patronising. Done casually in the vestry without even realising that anything is at stake, it can be patronising to the extent of being insulting.

The aesthetic ambiguities in the Torrance position struck home in my existential situation. More significantly, in the second half of the dogmatic odyssey which has been his life, he has in recent decades launched a daring assault on what he has rightly perceived as in our age the citadel of objectivity: science. He has over many years advanced with Christological trumpets blaring, to demolish the walls of scientific Jericho. He has written about science and religion as if, virtually single-handed, he could synthesise the new worlds of quantum physics with the images of Christ contained in the New Testament, the Patristic theologians, and the covenant theology of the reformers. Unhappily for synthesis, and for the stimulus this solo effort supplies to anyone concerned for the stripping away of triviality from late 20th Century theology, once the smoke of battle clears, the campaign to synthesise sometimes appears more like a mission to colonise: I suppose the same is true of the attitude of many theologians to music. They identify the enemy - 'sentimental froth'. Then they feel entitled to place it under pro-consular theological protection backed up by the tanks of objective criteria. All this brilliant activity is bristling with inherent ambiguity. But whereas less dogmatic theologians do not deny ambiguity, but affirm it, neo-calvinists and evangelicals tend to deny ambiguity, while inevitably practising it. Evangelicals will agree, in effect, with Torrance's view that theology is not only able to beat art and science in revealing the truth. They will agree with him that theology actually leads us to the truth, because it deals with what is objectively given - God revealed in Christ.

To amplify the point, I have to pull another autobiographical curtain. Torrance sweeping an audience into his world-view in the realm of ideas could be a thrilling and, at the emotional level, a liberating experience. Where it becomes exposed is when the psychic energy is transferred into the making of judgements in areas where the author has no particular expertise. As I am repeatedly saying in one way or another, music is too big a matter for expert musicians to be the sole arbiters of what in it is authentic, but I urge this democracy of interest to enable doors to be opened, not shut. The moment I decided enough was enough was when I heard Torrance deliver definitive *dicta* on the status of Mozart, Bach, and Beethoven, in which Beethoven, spiritually speaking, came bottom. Torrance was following Karl Barth in putting Mozart top of the league because he accepts his creaturely existence; he is the pagan who accepts the created order, the world as it is in objective truth. Mozart accepts, in Barth's phrase, "The State of Affairs" - a phrase which, if you follow the story line of Mozart operas, has more than one possible connotation.

Bach, however, in this view, was guilty of spiritualising faith, indeed of that most heinous of 20th Century sins, religionising it, making it a matter of subjective human religiosity, the soul's egocentric quest in the proud realm of human ideals, when it should lie in the humble acceptance of a given reality. Bach, then, does not distinguish himself in the view of this kind of objective theology. But Ludwig van Beethoven flunks it altogether, not even a Beta minus for him. Beethoven, said Torrance, reaches arrogantly up to Heaven and tries to grasp God: his Ninth Symphony is simply not on the menu for Christians. Tempted though one is to say to all this, simply, "Tosh!", that will not quite do. For buried in these judgements are half truths. Again, the colourful Torrentian daub of paint conveys an impressionistic picture which is recognisable. What does not work is the ideological judgement, the placing of the impression in a rigid logical system.

Yes, of course Beethoven sometimes storms Heaven. But that is a figure of speech, not an ideological programme. Beethoven also engages in ferocious struggles on earth, and plumbs depths in the subconscious - though not perhaps as manipulatively as, say, Wagner. But we also are now falling into the trap of generalising slogans! Who is this Beethoven? A man of whom, as in the case of Jesus, Pilate, and Paul, we actually know little as regards his interior life. What we do know are his compositions. Take, for example, the serenity of the Pastoral Symphony, or the Triple Concerto; and compare it with the darkness in Mozart's 'Don Giovanni' or 'Requiem'. Which composer in these works is accepting the created order and which is struggling beyond the grave? The stereotypes just don't fit.

As for the sketch of Bach as being so committed to a spiritual quest that he becomes unearthed, it is so remote from my experience that I have to give a personal thumbs down from the fairly earthed environment of an Intensive Care ward. A short number of years ago, I visited the Vale of Leven Hospital for a break from routine work under cover of a cardiac diversion of moderate magnitude. Under the pressure of getting my corporeal act together, I submitted to a number of mechanical aids which were in no sense natural to me. Some were more obviously necessary than others. I was in no position to contest wiring me up to information and action systems. What the heck, I thought, in for a penny, in for a pound. So I gave up the habit of a lifetime. I let my son buy me a Sony Walkman. With it he brought the Six Brandenburg Concerti of Bach. Someday a bright lad or lassie should get a Ph.D. of more value than most for doing detailed research into the therapeutic effects of different forms of music on various mental and physical states. Even within the limited category of classical orchestral music, the variation in the clinical effects produced by different composers was startling. I have to tell you that one composer, and one composer only, was of any value to me for the first crucial week. Guess who? That spiritually questioning *religioso*, 'unearthed' Johann Sebastian. Although the usual sedatives were applied and played their part, what gave me not only sleep, but contented sleep, accepting the very earthed order I was in, was Bach. What gave me a reasonably calm approach to the ups and downs of a threatened mind and body and the ins and outs of the hospital circus was Bach. What gave me a substantial hope of re-entering a normal world - I stress substantial hope - was Bach. I can vouch for the good effect. But was it achieved by bad means?

Again, I will resist the temptation to say, "Tosh!". What Bach contributed to my condition was the opposite of a vague religiosity. The Brandenburgs worked because of their composer's exactitude of craftmanship. In his time Bach was known not as a spiritual quester but as an organ-builder and organist. He was a practical man. He was also of course, a genius, but the genius worked through mathematically poised patterns of an almost micro-chip order of precision. Yet it never sounds predetermined: thus the genius. To be as precise as I can, the miracle which I felt to re-order the cells, molecules, and atoms of my entire biological ecosystem emanated from an achievement by an ordinary sort of church musician and organ builder dead over two centuries ago: namely that, like Ezekiel over a couple of thousand years before in his vision of wheels, he saw that the divine is not only as complex as the latest computer, but infinitely more so, so it can comprehend the complexity of our predicaments, and has spare intelligence to deal with us in a sufficiently relaxed way as to laugh, cry, sing, dance and generally go whoopee.

After ten days in hospital, I felt strong enough, out of interest, to bring some variety into my musical diet: I tried some 19th Century Romantic music. My organism reacted emetically as if invaded by a toxic substance. Even Brahms was too heavily emotional. Mozart almost made it. But I only felt at ease again when I went back to Bach's union of the lyrical and mathematical, the subjective and objective, the brilliantly coordinated symmetries of counterpoint and fugue together with the almost jazz-like jauntiness of syncopated dance: in a phrase, his ordered freedom or - better, perhaps - freedom in order. Mozart did come next. Once out of hospital, the order in freedom of his enchanted world brought me into increasingly relaxed dialogue with the emotional complexities of the post-hospital environment - family life, road traffic, social encounters, and eventually work. This mental rehabilitation was like a speeded up run through history, catching up with the accelerating pace at which emotional life is lived. By the time that process was complete, I was ready to engage again with more romantic composers of whom it might be said they were egocentric spiritual questers, as charged. My heart, metaphorically, and my psychosomatic system, practically, was now able to take their brazenly emotional assaults on my subconscious.

I hope I have shown in this simple way that Bach was good, not bad, and that he was good not because he was religious, but because he was wired into an earthbound reality, to the exact and exacting circumstances of an organism in peril which, under pressure, needed clear and absorbable information - that is, truth - about the potential of order out of chaos. In other words, Bach strikes a balance between the objective and the subjective which, because it is true, heals and liberates. One simple word for such a blessing is indeed beauty - so perhaps old Keats is right. But I have no wish to swing into the opposite error of saying that romantics are untruthful, because in that life-dance of the organism between the subjective and the objective, they tilt the rhythm one way rather than another. In circumstances quite different from the one I was in, the romantic drive of a Richard Strauss or a Berlioz may ring true for a person facing a daunting but exhilarating challenge in love, life or work. While another, in profound gloom, may find Tchaikovsky, wearing his sobbing heart on his sleeve, is able to assist by sharing his or her solitary desolation. In passing, I wish now I had carried my experiment into the 20th Century. Would Stravinsky's glittering neo-classical patterns have been as calming as Bach, and Shostakovich's equally contrapuntal passion have been as destabilising as Tchaikovsky's? Or is Torrance right (in this respect), to identify in Bach an extra spiritual ingredient which brought comfort?

I may now regret the limits of the experiment, but my motivation was actually to survive, not to fill gaps in lectures of whose future existence I was not aware! Lest a cardiac crisis should seem an unsafely narrow experience upon which to base a view of Bach, I switch now to another kind of critical experience. In the fifties, while I still had the stamina for it, I played my part in supporting the early harbingers of the Edinburgh Festival Fringe. Even in those halcyon days, the ordeal was no less than now; the stacking chairs no softer, the foetid halls no larger, the performances no more reticent. I attended one play in a dank space with a roof and walls, off a Royal Mile close. The absence of a stage defined the experience as theatre in the round; we sat in a circle. My two companions were Douglas Templeton and Roland Walls, Presbyterian and Anglican theologians respectively. Suddenly we were concussed by warlike music from amplifiers powered for Nuremberg. Smoke canisters were exploded. Out of the smoke appeared the cast. I think they were the cast. For an hour in between machine gun fire they ran about and shouted. At the interval, Roland sighed deeply and said, "I have dispeace. May we go?" It was but a five minute walk to St. Giles, where I was still assistant organist. I set them down in its enfolding shadows, while I went up to the loft and played Bach. Healed, we took coffee nearby and parted for the night. J.S.B. had won again.

That story, though historically true and fitting neatly in this context, carries an inbuilt snag. It fits too neatly. It confirms the stereotyped view of Bach as sucky blanket material for distressed persons of religious inclination; and once again it appears to suggest that, from the religious perspective, truth is to be found in the classical rather than the romantic muse. To balance any such impressions, I move to Sheffield for an anecdote which, by one of these serendipities which makes submitting to autobiographical compulsion occasionally worthwhile, involved exactly the same trio of participators: so some of the elements are present for a controlled experiment in musical psychotherapy. The scene is a wet night in Sheffield's city centre. We are standing in a queue at the bus-stop, and as in early technicolor movies, yellowing streetlights reflect moodily in pavement puddles. I forget whether Walls, Templeton or I said it, but the sentiment was that it was as well to have a preview of hell before one actually gets there. This was a comment, not on Sheffield, but on the Hallé Orchestra concert we had just left. Barbirolli had conducted performances which, sumptuous with string tone in the classical first half, had alchemised in the romantic second half into structures of crystal clarity. Berlioz is a one-off composer. His orchestration, like his harmony, is like no-one else's. He breaks the rules of orchestration, exposing instruments at heights and depths away off their usual pitch and' timbre. The results in the last two movements of the 'Symphonie Fantastique' have a crystalline cruelty. 'The March to the Scaffold', for example, ends with an icily bright chord on the brass which alchemises the major key into something more horrible than a minor chord. However, it was of 'The Witches Sabbath' which, in every sense, winds up the work, that we were thinking. It is a wicked brew, with increasingly bucolic squeakings, cacklings, chatterings, and brayings whirling through black holes into what is assumed to be red-hot devilry; yet, actually under Barbirolli it had been white-hot, or red-cold, like being burned by ice. This was no easy-going descent into chaos. Barbirolli treated the Berlioz score with exact respect. Every note was given its hellish space. The whole ghastly farrago was set out with austere despatch. The conductor, usually warmly expansive, was as clinically serious as one of the scientists unveiling the first nuclear bomb. The consequence was a scary performance. It was as if Sir John had peered into the Berlioz abyss, seen it as real, and was passing it on to us with a health warning.

I never tire of quoting Karl Barth as saying Christians should start with the state of affairs. If you become aware of another dimension, you are closer to apprehending reality, and whether the medium is a classical or a romantic composer, or whether the subject matter falls into overtly objective or subjective categories, is irrelevant. What matters is to be truthful. And the truth mattered to each of us that night. Douglas Templeton and I were visiting Roland Walls, who was conducting in Sheffield an experiment in preparing Anglican candidates for the priesthood. He was preparing them for the truth. For some months they worked in industry, and stayed in industrial workers' homes. Then they spent time in a small community with Roland. He has been a remarkable priest, monk, scholar, and teacher, who, later in small communities in Roslin and Cumbrae, and in retreats and colleges everywhere, has, sometimes with humour, always with meditative discipline, for generations lifted the events and parables of the New Testament existentially off the page. But in Sheffield, then, his job was to test the young men in his care, almost to destruction. He selected those churches in the Sheffield area which were most run-down and out of touch with society, the numinous - anything - and sent the ordinands to worship there. After their months in industry and in the homes of people who found the church irrelevant, this was a devastating experience, and some simply gave up the idea of becoming clergy. The negative aspect of this work worried Roland. And he was not entirely easy (though he joked about it) at putting the mark of Cain on the churches to be visited. Douglas Templeton, now a most subtle and underestimated New Testament scholar, was also going through a vocationally uncertain period, as I was. So we were a group ripe for truth, a structured truth, something we could live on, whether it was pleasant or otherwise. For us, therefore, facing differing degrees of disorder in our lives and beliefs, Berlioz was extremely orderly - his delineation of hell was, to us, relatively objective. Romantic? Classical? Do these terms mean anything?

The Barthian objective theologian is joined by the post-war neo-Barthian theologian who follows Bonhoeffer in saying that Man has come of age and need no longer manoeuvre God into the gaps of human need. This theological school respected music which was strong, objective, clear; it had little time for weak music which pandered to human neurosis. Therefore, by extension, subjective neurotic music is anathema in Christian worship where we meet to get caught up in the truth of God's strength and Christ's liberating grace, not to wallow round indulgently in the murky shallows of our human needs. I think most of this analysis is misconceived, but it has been a fashionable misconception among the opinion-formers in church music for a couple of generations, as part of that anti-*kitsch* reaction against Victorian sentimentality to which I referred in Chapter Two. I concede that Victoriana at its most romantically unbridled led to some music and words whose emotional lifestyle was liable to finish up in an intensive care ward. But, despite that concession, the thesis that it is wrong to express and respond subjectively to human need, even sick need, rests on the assumption that we are designed to be free from need, and that we are most truly ourselves when we are most free from our needs. I know that in non-Western spirituality - Buddhism, for example - the unshackling of one's soul from human needs and desires is a cardinal spiritual aim. But I am not yet a paid-up Buddhist. Do not, however, Western monks and nuns strive for this? I am not yet a paid-up monk or nun! Do not those who practise secular meditation, do not even those taking adult evening classes in *yoga*, seek the liberating tranquillity of unstressed plateaux of acceptance? My friends will not be surprised to hear that sitting cross-legged is not an activity that greatly occupies my evenings. Are not executives now told to practise stress-freeing finger exercises while their fellow drivers paw the ground at traffic lights? Well, I am no longer an executive, and when I was, I found it simpler to play Mozart and Tchaikovsky on the car radio. But what, finally, about wonderful old ladies whose beautiful lives, all passion spent, are devoted to pruning the roses, feeding the hungry - grandchildren or cats - and fulfil their psyches by singing sweetly in the church on Sundays? I do not expect to be an old woman, beguiling apotheosis though that would be. But in any case most of the wonderful old women I have met have been wonderful precisely because of the blazing egocentricity of their vitriolic passions, firm opinions, and energetic wickedness. Indeed, isn't that the point? If the thesis is that Man and Woman have come of age, then we don't need to evacuate them of all that makes them maddeningly, dangerously, gloriously individual. They can stand on their own deformed feet, their own feet of clay. They can be as they are. That is how they can receive God.

Human beings need to need. They are built in such a way that they need to need God, or whatever it is that the word God is taken to represent. But also, they need to need the whole range of emotions music can offer. Church music is no exception. This is by no means an academic question. It was because the editors of CH3 - the last Church of Scotland hymn book - had swallowed whole the implication that to have come of age is to boast hygienic good taste that they were programmed to be suspicious of hymns that were too subjective, and that is why favourite tunes and hymns were left out. As a result the church had a hymn book which was in some respects deeply untrue to the reality of people's emotional situation. People's emotional situation is sometimes this: AAARGH!

To sum up what I have been saying: if you're going to try to be genuinely objective about reality, then you must be objective about the human condition, and that means you have to be objective about the subjective, and accept it in a big way. In which case you may as well be generous in your acceptance and wallow, from time to time, in the Big Tune; for the truth may be that the Divine has a Big Heart which enjoys a good wallow as well as the next woman - or man. To say other is to suggest that come-of-age love, human or divine, is so sophisticated that a good cry is not allowed. And my reply to that is not, "Tosh!" I will just say, ever so quietly: I beg to disagree.

That, I hope, is to conclude the difficult and negative part of this chapter: the case for the defence of the subjective, its right to exist. I am content to rest that and to proceed now to a more interesting enquiry: exploration of the worlds of objective magic that lie ready to be discovered in the depths of the subjective. At which cross-over point, we will junk these terms altogether. Over the bridge they go, into the ravine of discarded jargon. We are now able to travel lighter. We are free to enter the territory of... Ambiguity. What a let-down! Ambiguity? Yes, for nothing is more exciting than this. It is the alchemy of both life and art that reality can be experienced both in one way and in another way. Real freedom is to choose not between right or wrong, but between real and unreal; and no system of rules exists, certainly not in the worlds of art and music, that can guarantee to sort that out.

In late 1990, I was returning from Israel. At 37,000 feet over the Island of Rhodes, the entertainer and composer Donald Swann was sitting beside me in the El Al jumbo, and he was writing out for me the words of a number of his songs. What made me ask him for these was the fact that the night before,

Donald was sitting at the piano 200 yards from the border across which was the Palestinian part of Jerusalem which had been having trouble. It was the night of the Jewish Sabbath. We were in Jerusalem, the holiest city in the world. That day I had stood in the Bethlehem cave where Jesus is reckoned to have been born. We were at the crossroads of geopolitical time and space, secular history and salvation history. And what, to his audience of Jews, Arabs, and other races did Donald sing? 'Mud, mud, glorious mud.' Ah, but that must have been a one-off, what else did he sing? Well, 'The Gnu Song', 'The Transport of Delight' (the London Omnibus Song), and the song about the disappearing slow lines of Britain's trains.

He also gave us a song he had just written, a pearl of a song called, 'The Sign of the Reed', with a strong Eastern influence. He finished with the famous mournful Russian folk-song about the camels - that quintessential non-story about a desert where absolutely nothing happens - but sung by Donald with such ferocity that one camel appearing over the horizon, then a second, then a third, then a fourth, and so on... then one camel moving off, then a second one, then a third... then one camel having a sore foot etc... becomes a drama to beat into a cocked hat the Gulf crisis and the Arab-Israeli volcano threatening round the corner.

I would not tell this merely to squeeze anecdotal pips out of a trip. The whole situation struck me as a bizarre and therefore telling example of the kind of emotional and cultural cocktail that defies the attempt by any system of theology or aesthetics to put liturgy in a cage. Here in the religious and political cockpit of the world, people of mixed races and beliefs laughed and cried as Donald sang. The lament for the passing of the rural railway, sad as any English elegy, made us laugh. The Russian camel drama, taking the mickey out of the desert myth, made us crease ourselves till we cried. His new setting of 'The Sign of the Reed', a key poem by the 12th Century poet, Rumi, brought an intense meditative stillness into the cabaret scene. It was a healing occasion, I would say a sacramental one, but I would challenge anyone to disentangle it in terms of objective or subjective reality.

I have been majoring in conductors as exemplars of different approaches to music-making, rather than on pianists, singers, or organists, because conductors have high and memorable profiles, because they are likely to be widely known to a cross-section of music lovers, and because they carry a subliminal metaphorical message about God's relationship to the orchestra of creation. I don't want to overdo that metaphor, because it is limited in scope: one needs many metaphors for God, of which composer is perhaps the most obvious. But there is another reason for using orchestral conductors as exemplars. They are oblique to the topic of church music. One can therefore make points of style or substance without immediately treading on the corns of church music practitioners, specially ones who, being alive, could sue me or at least cut me in the street.

However, I would like now, at whatever litigious risk, to move nearer home. Having, I hope, established that I am not enamoured of a right or wrong way of doing music nor of any overall philosophy which has *ex cathedra* authority in aesthetics or theology, it should be possible to describe differences without imputing value judgements. Which is just as well, for my goodness, are there differences? I have experienced them in the organ playing field, and I have experienced them there with maximum existentiality. I said organ playing field, and field is a good word, for what one experienced was two force fields coming from opposite directions and proceeding, it seemed, in immutably contradictory paths. I had two organ teachers and musical gurus. One was W.O. Minay, then organist in St. Cuthbert's in Edinburgh and teacher at Fettes, where I first encountered him. When I left Fettes I spent a further period assisting him at St. Cuthberts and continuing with organ tuition. The second was Herrick Bunney, whom I assisted at St. Giles for many fascinating years and who took over my organ tuition. Before I explain the differences in the approach of these two mentors to matters musical, it might be useful to apply, not a preparatory anaesthetic, because that would deaden awareness, nor an unguent, as if negative scarring was anticipated, nor even a tourniquet, as if escalating blood pressure might boil over, but an emollient, in the shape of stating what I found them to have profoundly in common. Their common characteristics included integrity, sensitivity, warmth, adoration of the organ, and deep caring for the essence of what it is that is going on when human souls gather for worship. That is to say that in most things that matter they were as brothers. If they had not been I would not have given allegiance to both. But in most things musical their styles were so different that chalk and cheese acquire by comparison the identity of twin substances.

The polarisation of their musicianship was prefigured by their bodies and personalities. Bill Minay was small, with a sharp face belying a deep Lancashire drawl. When he spoke one became aware of a dangerous wit overlaid with the courtesy of a brilliant lad who has learned to suffer fools with resignation. As a result of his failure, like Professor Sidney Newman, to genuflect to the Edinburgh music establishment, he went down there with the élan of a lead balloon; the fact that he just happened to be a genius being something which, if it did not entirely escape the attention of those musical panjandra, was assessed as a containable inconvenience. Those of us who turned up Sunday by Sunday at St. Cuthberts were treated to unforgettable musical experiences. That huge yet strangely muted church (now vandalised by partition), became for me a liturgical Bayreuth, where one did not only hear and see, but experience, its enveloping world of cloud-capped mystery. In passing, why have those who worshipped at St. Cuthberts been so pampered down the years? Did they make some Faustian pact with the Devil? If so, the nemesis will be formidable, to pay for such magic as the preaching of George MacLeod at his Titanic prime and the majesty of Adam Burnet, a Prospero of preachers who ransacked the treasures of scripture, prayer book, and English literature to weave a magisterial spell. On top of all that, a quarter of a century of Minay's organ playing was more than a West End congregation could possibly have earned by good works. Their faith, of course, may have been prodigious. Or, *au contraire*, their sinning so fearful as to require the outpouring of all this truly amazing grace.

My wife and I visited the real Bayreuth years later, to experience, in its multi-dimensional majesty, the Ring Cycle, so I do not make the comparison lightly. Just as in that custom built Wagner auditorium one waits for the orchestral sound to be born in another world before stealing out of the cave-like pit, so as an emotionally hungry teenager I sat hugging myself in St. Cuthbert's, waiting for that first throb of the pedal, tinkle of the flutes, splash of the strings, carillioning of the mixtures, or pirouetting of the trumpets, to announce the beginning of an hour and a half of astonishment. Even better, it might be the sudden patterning of a Bach Prelude and Fugue, or a noble work by Rheinberger, Reubke, Reger, Karg-Elert or Franck that burst out of the chancel and flooded up the nave, its shapes dancing up and down like the shadows of a thousand candles flickering against the walls of an Aladdin's Cave. Minay was generous. No vertiginous descent from a hasty last minute chat in the vestry to a five minute voluntary covering entry of choir and clergy. This was an organ recital for the gods, a preparation for mysteries, a sustained incantation at the gate of high seriousness. By the time the minister arrived, one was ready for great things to happen. How lucky I was (I now realise) that in Adam Burnet one was not disappointed. But even when lesser men occupied the prayer desk and pulpit, the way Minay accompanied the hymns kept the dramatic pulse alive.

This was romantic organ playing of a prodigious order. The little man with the caustic wit was subsumed in a giant. The beanstalk was transfigured into a ladder of gold, hymns were excursions for angels, Jack became Jesus indeed, and Paradise was here. Nothing could more decisively appear to break the Torrance taboo, for was it not obvious that Minay had knocked at Heaven's gate and midwifed God into this Edinburgh mausoleum of a 2,000 year old cult?

And, if so, how?

I have called this chapter 'Mining for Gold'. This was a gloss on 'Minaying for Gold'. Minay linked earth and heaven, not by some arrogant gesture skywards, but by humble digging downwards. He was a deep seam miner hacking away at the coal face of other men's inspirations. I do not mean he was unaware of his own worth. He had been a brilliant young student, a pupil of Vaughan Williams, a youthful organist in Exeter Cathedral who later built a great choir at Wigan Parish Church, and helped Norman Cocker to build a new organ at Manchester Cathedral. He was frequently asked to give organ recitals on the Third Programme and at least once gave a recital on the Festival Hall organ on London's South Bank. But the reason all this counted for little in the world of Edinburgh reputations was that he himself counted it for little. He saw his as a humble art, a craft, a service, to work away at the practical business of revealing the detail of others' compositions and of the words and music of hymns and psalms. He worked away at truth in the inner parts. Every phrase had to be dug out, assessed, evaluated, given its true worth in relation to its neighbour, given room to breathe, shaped, cleaned up, brightened, clarified, sprung into action, ennobled, redeemed, transfigured.

I'm talking hard work. I'm talking the kind of genius which is 90% perspiration. In terms of Bach, he was a follower of Albert Schweitzer, who gave the first part of his life to studies in philosophy and music, and had dug deep into the phrasing of Bach's organ works. As a result of unremitting delving into the intricacies of phrasing, Minay often took a Bach prelude, and specially a fugue, significantly slower than other organists. It seemed sometimes dangerously slow, as if the surgeon was taking the vital organ out of the body for close inspection, and breathing might stop. But always the body was put together again with such scrupulous attention not only to detail but to the overall original vision, that when it grew to its full height, took up its bed and strode around the church, it was a resurrected body, a miniature cosmos glittering with transfigured life. The principal technical means employed in this resurrecting surgery was the percussive touch. By the use of staccato, alternating with legato, Minay shaped phrases as if bowing a stringed instrument. This was striking enough in letting air into treble and bass parts. When it was applied through all the inner parts of a complex fugue, the effect was staggering, like seeing an ancient mosaic in bold relief after the grime of centuries has been cleaned off.

Those of us who simply do not have such talent or scholarship may feel we have little to learn here, because we are just not up to it, but there are lessons even for us. First, worship deserves the absolute best we can offer. The symbolic bleak Sunday morning in February of which I often speak is, in its import, as much an assignation with destiny as the opening concert of a Festival in front of Royalty and the world's *cognoscenti*. And here, I reconcile the Byronic Tom Torrance with the Beethovian musician, for I once heard Professor Norman Porteous describe attending an evening service at Alyth when Torrance was the young minister in that small farming town. There were in the church a handful of country folk with no outward sign of enthusiasm or even interest. Torrance delivered a sermon of blazing evangelical sincerity and exegetical magnitude, a towering inferno of the kerugma, as if by that one act of dedicated service to the Word, he could save the world. And then the handful of country folk woke up and went home to their supper. So Minay played. And so all of us can do our absolute best with whatever talent we have.

Second, as I'm sure Tom Torrance did for every sermon, Bill Minay did his homework for each service as if it were a final examination. Skimping fresh preparation for a Bach fugue he had played all his life would have been as foreign to his musical conscience as Chicken Chow Mein to his Lancashire palate. This is to say that for Minay every act of worship was an eschatological reality. At every moment, last things, ultimate assessments, were involved.

Third, he gave us as many treats before and after as if we had emptied our wallet for Jessye Norman or the Berlin Philharmonic. I'm not suggesting we can all supply such treats, but some of us can; and at least clergy should enable musicians who have talents to use them.

Fourth, he did not patronise hymns and psalms. Upon each item of praise he lavished the same rigorous attention to detailed phrasing as he did on a great organ work. He studied the words, the syntax, the dramatic profile of the story line, the inner harmonic potential of the tune. And he did this as seriously in the case of a weak-ish Victorian hymn as with a powerful classic of praise - indeed, reflecting St. Paul, the weak tune was given extra attention, and transfigured into an apotheosis of itself. The hymn, in its whole performance, became a tone poem, coloured in with bold use of registration, harmonic variations, and, when appropriate, zig-zag cross rhythms.

Again, we may not all have such talents, but we can all take the praise list a great deal more seriously than most of us do. We can at the very least not treat it as a routine matter. There are more detailed lessons one could learn from the Minay technique, but as this is not a workshop, these must be left on one side, to leave intact the principle that this kind of craftsmanship embodied: namely, that truth is released when personal commitment - the subjective reality - is placed at the service of detail in the context of the infinite... in the context of so-called objective reality.

This is where the romantic musician is digging at the identical golden seam, deep underground, to which the classical musician is attending. God, the gods, the numinous, whatever name you use, is not stuck up there (wherever one thinks 'up there' is). He, they, it, is incarnate here in the travail of good work, honestly done; but that good work has to be really good, the best we can do, plus a little more, plus, if the truth be told, a costly amount more.

What then, is left to say about Herrick Bunney that is not a wounding anti-climax? Ah, that is the amazing grace that I experienced that has left me at least in music, a permanently humbled spirit. Having moved up the road to assist in the organ loft of the High Kirk of St. Giles, I came under the tutelage of an organist who in detail performed almost entirely differently, but, in result, was equally inspirational. His personality was different, to start with. Where Minay was small and appeared diffident, Bunney, though not tall, appeared so; if not actually swashbuckling, his confident bearing suggested a hint of buckle here, and a dash of swash there - hints which materialised with electric effect when in his early days he magnetised big choirs like the Edinburgh Royal Choral Union. The Bunney scale of arm-waving made Malcolm Sargent look like a sedated sandbag.

Over the years, Herrick scaled down his conducting to match his increasing commitment to small choirs like the University Singers, and this was an outward paradigm of the inner pathway of his musical evolution. Whereas Minay built up from micro to macro, Bunney explored down from macro to micro. As I said, there is more than one way to skin a cat; Bunney's instinct was to go for the big cat, the jaguar, but because he was also a dedicated craftsman, his life in music became an odyssey towards the miniature. Musically, he journeyed from gold Cadillac to the diamond on the tie pin. To be specific, in matters choral, he began with heroic attempts to spark fire from huge choirs like the Choral Union. (It sometimes needed heroism: during the interval of the New Year 'Messiah', the choir decanted into the rearward corridors to eat pies out of paper bags; and I recall with delicious horror the way the eyes of the same choir stood out on stalks when Beecham, conducting a lacklustre afternoon rehearsal for 'L'Enfance du Christ', silkily enquired, "What did you have for lunch, Ladies, haggis?"). To be historically fair, the Bunney windmill did breathe life, sometimes even passion, into that amply bosomed choral organism. But in his odyssey towards inner truths unavailable on that scale, Bunney evolved a quite different style with chamber choirs. Fleet of foot and elegantly toned contrapuntal singing of motets, cantatas, and notably an annual Easter performance of the 'St. Matthew Passion', produced exquisitely paced performances, intimate, yet of deep religious urgency. When Bunney burst on to the Edinburgh scene in 1946, his heroic capacity to throw the organ around brought an unfamiliar excitement to Presbyterian worship. It wasn't a brutal heroism. He had a Barbirolli-like panache, which could, like Barbirolli, also suffuse with delight the English numinosity of Elgar and Howells. His sense of occasion energised his playing of Handel and the modern French school alike. St. Giles has many services which are dubbed special, spawning processions and recessions as to the manner born. This involves the congregation in much sitting around waiting for the next parade to appear at the West Door. The Bunney sparkle transformed these choreographic wastelands into *coups de théâtre*.

A tedious crocodile of municipal pomposity would become a *corps de ballet* sweeping up the aisle to a fusillade of Vierne or Vidor. The geriatric meandering of a *cortège* of enthistled knights would become a noble sward of surging green on which Bunney improvised a Messiaen-like paean. Like Minay, he was a brilliant improviser; but whereas Minay began with a detailed idea and built outwards, Bunney started from an impressionistic canvas and worked the detail in.

But it would be misleading to convey an impression that the Bunney organistic brilliance lay in surface impressions. His commitment was to the secret heart of music as of worship. He just believed, as a matter of musical judgement, that it is the whole picture that counts, and you start with the impetus that requires, in tempo and colour. He has more than once given recitals of the whole corpus of Bach's organ works, and as keen a critic as Erik Routley thought it was as majestic an unveiling of the vast Himalayan landscape of Bach as could be experienced this side of Elysium. So the ambiguity is resolved, or is it? Bunney's Bach was not Minay's Bach, but both were Bach. The answer is that there is room for both, for what is a composition bequeathed to us by a master? It is not like a mass produced car off a factory line, every performance a clone of every other. It is a door opened into other worlds, and each person may step through it, in different directions. The basis of the Bunney technique was a flowing legato which sought the architecture of the whole. The basis of the Minay technique was the rhythmic staccato which liberated the inner intricacies and let the accumulating counterpoint build the edifice afresh.

So: legato or staccato, what is truth? Where is truth? When is truth? How do we get there, we who are neither expert diggers at the underground coal face, nor climbers of musical mountains? I will let you into a secret. Having been hundreds of times in the organ loft with both gurus, I can tell you what they were doing when they were not playing. They were listening. For both were explicit in their appreciation of craftsmanship in the pulpit, when it occurred. And both were critical of its absence if it was absent. No sermon, no prayer, escaped their concentrated attention. They knew, how I don't know, I suppose it was in their bones, that for Beauty to be whole, Truth must be indivisible. If the work in the pulpit was shoddy, superficial, meretricious, or pretentious, they felt their craft demeaned.

In Chapter Three, I described an Easter morning service in Durham Cathedral when, after a remarkable sermon by the Bishop, the cathedral organist sent the last two hymns into orbit. When I recounted this experience to Bishop David Jenkins, he said that, while he could not be sure what was in the organist's mind at that moment, it was undoubtedly the case that "James listens to sermons".

Who says preaching doesn't matter any more?

Bill Minay is in his eighties now, and Herrick Bunney in his seventies. Both are still musicians of the utmost distinction, but the prime of their careers is in the past. Is it another case of there were giants in those days? No, I'm glad to say, great organists and choir trainers follow. To mention but a handful, Andrew Armstrong and George McPhee, once Herrick's assistants, shower fireworks over lofty naves and chancels. Richard Galloway, son of my late Peterhead organist, the magnificent Tom Galloway, sparkles at Stirling. John Langdon, a romantic organist with the precision of Minay and the panache of Bunney, is a rising star who takes as defiant a risk in the humblest hymn as in a Berlioz bonanza; and in my own Helensburgh church, Walter Blair has for the nineteen years I have worshipped there made me leave every service with my heart singing, as the *bravura* of his playing fresh minted every Sunday sweeps through the service. Church music's magic is not dead. We have everything still to play for. And for digging and climbing to proceed, we need not only experts of their calibre. We of lesser talents have our specific opportunities.

The one essential thing is to believe that it matters. Like Tom Torrance in that half empty church in Alyth long ago, it is because God is there that we do it. What He sees as truth is not these fragments that we see. He sees us whole and He hears the inner parts. It is He who resolves all the ambiguity, reconciles bone and marrow, alchemises my dross to his gold, makes Omega Alpha, and recreates the world.

Chapter Seven

ALL THAT GLITTERS

This book is not about music as such. It is about church music. To be even more specific, it is about normal church music. This may come as a surprise to some. I have, they may say, covered nearly all the inner and outer archipelagos of human experience currently under the purview of Caledonian Macbrayne and all creation, with the exception of normal religious music. I think I must bat this suggestion gently back, for, while I have sought to broaden the concept of what church music is ultimately about, I have also repeatedly said that in its practical manifestation it characteristically boils down to concrete *minutiae* like deciding the speed of a given hymn, at a given point in a given morning service in St. Trad. by the Co-op on a given bleak Sunday in February. So, while I have located the macro aspect of church music in the broadest sweep of divine energy and human culture, I have identified its micro essence in the hymn. In Scotland, at any rate, I have suggested, if we get the hymns right, we have a good chance of getting most other things, if not absolutely right, at least not terribly wrong.

But on what basis can one discuss, let alone judge, what is relatively right and relatively wrong - specially when what I have mainly offered is anecdote? Even when I attempted to deal with the age-old conundrum of objectivity and subjectivity, I did so in a highly subjective frame by recalling personal experiences at my theological college. But even to mention the words subjective and objective is enough to make me shudder as I throw them back over my shoulder, because I have no wish to reincarnate, even to rebut it, the neo-Calvinist claim to have access to objective language; a language which has been claimed not only to be objective about God, the World, Science, and why spiders climb anti-clockwise out of the bath, but a language so objective that it can rationally evaluate the spiritual status of great composers like Bach, Mozart, and Beethoven. I declined to agree with the implications of such criteria, but they are highly serious criteria, whether in Reformed Continental liturgy, in Scottish circles of liturgical renewal, or in the landscape of Torrance theology. The reason all this mattered somewhat was that the editors of CH3 seemed to me, on the internal evidence of that hymn book, to have been hi-jacked by this anti-subjective heavy mob, and thus to have tilted CH3 away from the emotional centre of most of the Scots who engage in normal worship. Faced with this intellectual Rolls-Royce, I felt that the only way to stop it in its tracks was to crash into it with all the verbal energy of which my rattling mini-brain is capable, and this explains the *débris* of the vocabulary of subjectivity and objectivity that litters recent pages.

But now, I must begin to address myself to some of the practical questions which, surely, any pontificator on church music might be expected to regard as his agenda. After all, this is not a recondite topic. Have I not just said it boils down to what we do on Sunday mornings? In which case, the core of my response should be an answer. I should say what we should do on Sunday mornings. Well, yes and no. Those who have followed me thus far will realise that everything I have offered in anecdote, argument, or demonstration has been dedicated to a rather different purpose. Yes, of course, practical questions require practical answers, but as any military strategist, political fixer, football coach, parent, teacher, doctor, or engineer knows, the primary job, before hazarding an answer, even an experimental answer, is to establish the core of the problem. Thereafter, as I have also repeatedly said, it is up to others, working across a wide range of situations, to perceive solutions for each time and place.

What I think I owe to people who care about those matters is not a manual of tactical devices on the ground, but a war strategy. Possibly the word 'war' is inappropriate. Even if some solutions may appear drastic in certain local conditions, it is to be hoped that implacable hostility will not be the motivation, a scorched earth policy the means, nor a legacy of bitterness the result. Yet a strategy of peace sounds wet. Let us just say: a strategy. I will not however, entirely resist the temptation to offer a specific tactical proposal or two. Indeed, before I conclude, I am going to lay a golden egg. I was going to call it a golden rule, but that would be to contradict my thesis that not a lot is absolutely wrong, and not a lot is absolutely right; and therefore that there are not a lot of absolute rules. Let's not, at this late stage, get sunk by semantics. There are rules of thumb. Call them rules if you will, but in relation to the imperatives of musical and spiritual inspiration, they have the status that details of hygiene in the journeys of the tribes of Israel have in relation to the majestic ideals enshrined in the vision of Sinai - which we call commandments, but are in fact inspirational encapsulations of ideals.

I have suggested that freedom and truth are basic categories which transcend gaps of generations, cultures, centuries, fashions. If in worship we do not fly free of the various cages that trap us in our multi-layered lives, then why go to church? I know that for committed people there are other admirable reasons, many of which, being decoded, amount to this or that form of stoicism. But it is a worry, increasingly voiced, that people are voting with their feet. They are staying away because they do not expect to find freedom of spirit in the hymn sandwich; so they call it 'boring'. This is frequently taken to be a straight rejection of the language of the pulpit, and, even more commonly, of the words and music of the traditional hymn. I am not at all convinced that it is as simple as that. My own diagnosis is that what we lack is the right kind of balance. Truthfulness in music is like truthfulness in life. It arises from and invests in a balance between emotional freedom and emotional control. A balance between emotional vulnerability (opening out completely) and emotional reticence (keeping one's emotions totally to oneself lest they should harm others). And a balance between logical intoxication (following through to the exhilarating conclusion this gift we have for rational construction), and logical scepticism - (submitting such constructions to testing to destruction).

Freedom, therefore, paradoxically, as Jesus said, is a narrow way. But the alchemy is this: if you try to follow that narrow way, yes, sometimes you fall off, but other times you fly into infinite space. How does one operate this balance? Who or what is the spiritual engineer in me in charge of this delicate balancing operation between all these potential force fields within me?

The super-engineer is not a super-id. Not a censor. Not a controller. He is the liberating *Logos*. The word that flies. The word, evolving through death and resurrection into spirit. Genius wriggles - or flies - past the Engineer. Genius is the bird that flies over the cuckoo's nest, but, though genius may, like Jack Nicholson, the hero of the film of that name, seem mad, true genius, unlike Nicholson, is still in control, or controlled or freed by the *Logos*, the word made Theatre in the stage of one human brain made, by this process, divine. We have access to this *via* art and the best religious music. But that need not stop us using the more normal route of our own mental and musical engineering. Most of our music cannot be at the the genius level, but it can obey the ground rules of freedom in balance, walking the tightrope of truth. Or, since we are not too keen on the implied rigidity of rules, we can say that our most ordinary music - our workaday hymns and songs - can open up to the fundamental rhythms of life, the rhythms of body, brain and soul. Such a balance of inner rhythm will not be in the business of *a priori* exclusion of any category of music. For example, a couple of weeks ago, I played a couple of Patrick Appleford hymns, one of which I thought was pretending to go somewhere while actually standing rooted to the spot, but the other of which did make a voyage of real interest. Yet both used the now somewhat cloying seeming harmonies and laborious syncopations of weak, early British musicals.

If the central aim of Christian liturgy is spiritual liberation, its central theme, in word and sacrament, is surely redemption. This too then must be central to its music; and by music one isn't referring to a static assembly of sound formations notated on paper and reproduced repetitively by performers, but to the way music is used. The word 'used' is itself, of course, suspect. Exploitation of music is different from its redemption. This is true of all music. It must be all the more true, therefore, of liturgical music, where the redemption is not only at the artistic level. At the liturgical level, where there is the possibility of an ultimate magic distilling concentrated spirit from aesthetic magic, we can envisage music not being used merely, but misused, as Christ was, abused as He was, and yet, through that redeeming energy process, the material being regenerated, redeemed, changed into something different, yet remaining essentially itself. That is the difference between redemption and exploitation. In exploitation, the original material is adapted, changed, forced into a convenient use, in such a way that it ceases to be, at heart, what it was.

A moment's reflection will show that this is not a matter of amount of change, on the surface level. You could slightly adapt a tune so that everyone would instantly say, "Oh, I know what that is", and yet by an over sophisticated, or a trivialising treatment, change its heart. And you can work on a tune so that it becomes a complex piece of music, not recognised easily, and yet feel that it has been allowed to keep its heart, its integrity. Somehow the message is the same, the authenticity is there, the authority of the author is not facilely undermined. In inspiring cases, the inner heart of the original has done more than survive. By a process of creative alchemy it has generated a magically exciting new world of possibilities. It is the humble mutant seed which has sprouted a forest where the birds of the air can find a home, and from which the spirits of the congregation can lift off and fly.

You can apply this principle right across the board to much simpler matters than arrangements and compositions, which, after all, only affect a minority, even of organists or choirmasters. Take something as basic as speed. A hymn may be brilliantly accompanied, faultlessly led by the choir, even sung by a well-drilled congregation - though that is less common - but if the speed, by being too fast or too slow, fights with the words of the hymn or the souls, brains, and bodies of the congregation, the material remains unredeemed. Equally, however, a hymn which sweeps a congregation off its feet by *bravura* playing and singing, may sweep it into a swoon rather than a voyage of exploration, and I would call that exploitation rather than redemption, emotional entrapment rather than spiritual freedom.

So: it is all quite difficult. Yes, it is. To do justice, let alone mercy, to our staple diet, is a musical and spiritual challenge of a high order. Yuri Bashmet, the Russian, and some say the world's greatest viola player, was twelve years old when he formed a rock band and soon was a teenage idol. But then he discovered classical music. The Times Review quotes him as saying, "For the first time I understood the difference: classical music puts questions to your soul; jazz music only to your brain and your body; and pop music only to your body."

That is an encapsulation of the musical odyssey worth bearing in mind; specially if we feel pressured by an imagined public demand to cheer up our worship with pop, rock, or jazz. That is not to be resistant to these forms, only to feel free not to lie down, roll over, and let current fashions engulf one: not, you may think, a likely danger for the time being.

I said, two chapters back, that our liturgy should be open to all creative activity in every form. I compared good jazz to Bach, and indicated a preference for proper rock, or pop, for that matter, to pale churchy reflections of the *genres*. I have kept saying that to be multi-principled is not to be unprincipled: that there is more than one way to skin a cat; and that in a multi-sensory and multi-tonal world, it is not only unnecessary, but perverse, to restrict methods and styles of musical expression. Putting it another way, an established church, such as the Church of Scotland, or the Church of England, is constitutionally in position to deal with the spirituality of the whole parish, the whole community, the whole nation. Its approach to music must, therefore, be eclectic, pragmatic, multi-principled. It cannot afford to be sectarian in music any more than in theology. To give a music analogy, despite the taste developed in recent decades for the 'baroque' organ, with a limited range of pure basic tones, most of the pipe organs in churches and cathedrals are still multi-stopped - to put it mildly. Does this mean they lack integrity? There's a big argument here. But even the player of a single-toned instrument who despises the organ because of its multiplicity of mechanically produced effects, might have paused, during the opening concert of the Glasgow Year of Culture, as John Langdon, on the restored organ in the Kelvingrove Art Gallery, crashed multi-tonal sound barriers with orchestra and choirs in the fanfares and echoing silences of the Berlioz 'Te Deum'.

Here we are, talking again about the organ. How so, in an era where we inhabit now a world with a plethora of alternative ear-tickling devices? Because, against the background of technical changes, it remains true that, apart from the human voice, the organ is the most obvious constant in public worship. In most worship buildings, still, it stands astrologically as the Leo of liturgy - proud, dominant, but capable also of totalitarian insensitivity which can cow an audience into submission, turning each worshipping soul into a decibelic dustbin. It is frequently the most pronounced visual as well as aural object. And it is the instrument most frequently hijacked by - or the instrument which most frequently jack-knifes - the race set apart to control, lead, or stimulate the musical element in worship; to the extent, indeed, that normally in Scotland, the musical minister is called, not that, nor even the master or mistress of music, but the organist.

In parenthesis, did you notice the phrase I slipped in there - "the musical minister"? In America, where they order things differently, if not always better, they do acknowledge the role of the ministry of music. Not that in Scotland a musical minister is uncommon. Look out for the signs in the Good Music Guide. They are: a spire or a tower, or a pointed roof, and a pulpit. There are thousands of them, and inside each is a musical minister. There are, you see, absolutely no unmusical ministers. For the clergy to admit that they are not musical is as unthinkable as to admit that they have no sense of humour, no valid opinion on sex, or no interest in football. For priests, the matter is a little different, but in the Reformed tradition, especially in Scotland, stained glass and kists of whistles having been rejected originally, there is an historical residue - the minister must retain control of the worship, therefore all that goes on, including the music, must have the guarantee of liturgical probity by being guided by his unfailing sense of what is musically appropriate. I am teasing, of course, well, a little. Many of the clergy have the sense to admit that they are not musicians. And to be fair, many others are more musical than the part-time organists who have generously placed their sincere but limited abilities at the disposal of the congregation.

Given this situation, it is obvious what one should do: pool all our talents openly, as I suggested in an earlier lecture. But it is easier said than done. Ministers and organists have good reason to be defensive. A man or woman who has worked long hours preparing carefully crafted material for prayers and sermon is not lightly to be persuaded to throw it all to the dogs by allowing into the service a disorderly concatenation of amateur noises, reducing a sensible script to a pig's breakfast. Nor is an organist who, whatever his limitations, has standards of musical integrity in his heart as well as his brain, to be casually suborned into letting shapeless self-expression sabotage musical traditions which still put questions to the souls of traditional worshippers.

Nevertheless, pool our talents we must, and this is where the balance comes in. And the test, remember, is whether the word, the living *Logos*, can be both earthed incarnate in people's lives, and then fly, in resurrection, liberating people's souls. Anything less is less than we need.

Now, then, it is time to lay my golden egg.

The egg that I am about to lay will be so naked as it lies there alone and unprotected, that some people will say: is that all? Yet others will say: you can't go that far! Which reaction it is will depend on the circumstance of the person reacting. A third sort of person I hope, will nod and say: yes, and about time, too. But like a hen getting hyped up for the big drop, now that I am about to reveal the practical product of all this aesthetic and liturgical brooding, I can hardly bear to part company with it, for fear of a shattering anti-climax. Suppose my ovoid, on breaking open on impact, should be found to be merely void? Before paralysis sets in, I'd better deliver.

The mystery object is PITCH.

Believe it or not, 'pitch' is not a metaphor. At long last, Mackenzie has landed. To spell it out in two words of one syllable: SING LOW. For this, a sweet chariot is not necessary. What is required is something even rarer: the steely determination of an organist and choirmaster to outface his or her choir. Why? Consider how the cookie crumbles. Generally speaking, the reason that hymns are pitched at the level they are is to accommodate four part singing. To push the tune down would evict sopranos, altos, tenors, and basses from their natural registers. Surely not to a serious extent? I can't be arguing that the lowering of a hymn by a semi-tone or even a tone would throw a professional choir completely off-balance? Ah no, but then that is not what I am suggesting.

Leaving aside the fact that only a minority of choirs are professional, when I say 'sing low', I mean sing very low. I'm talking not semitones and tones. I'm talking thirds, fourths, even fifths, yes, in some cases lowering the pitch by as much as half an octave. At this point, any choirmaster, organist, or chorister worth his salt is stopping his ears and walking through the door, or hurling this book across the room. While all those who are not practising musicians are shaking their heads and asking themselves, "So what? We sing lower. What's the big deal?"

The deal is this and it amounts to a fairly big re-shuffle of the church music pack. To lower the pitch of an average hymn by this much would be to put a strain on any choir singing it in harmony. Sopranos would lose their brilliance and would find some notes too low for comfort. Basses and contraltos might find a few notes virtually impossible. Tenors, I guess, would suffer least, if they were baritoney sort of tenors, and as tenors are in Scotland such a rare breed, that is just as well; but they also would lose their flexibility and brilliance, and would be far from pleased.

But, if lowering the pitch so drastically makes singing difficult, then why do it? But you see, it doesn't make singing as such more difficult, it makes singing in conventional four part harmony more difficult. It actually makes singing the tune, in unison, easier for the congregation. Could the choir then not sing the tune in unison? Indeed it could. But what, then, would be the point of having a choir?

There was silence in Heaven for half an hour.

When the silence ended, the stunned choristers of Heaven and Earth broke into a chattering of such unbridled indignation that would have drowned the noise made by all the starlings in the Glasgow dusk.

Let me put it not only plainly but bluntly. Let me call a spade a shovel. The average church choir is the main obstacle to a revival of church music.

No, that is too blunt. I will add a rider. The church choir, as presently constituted, used, abused, and exploited, and as aided and abetted by a hymnbook like CH3 which is designed not for congregations but for church choirs, is the main obstacle.

Which does leave open the possibility that the choir, constituted and used differently, might be not only useful to a revival of church music, but could be a redemptive and recreative force.

Why is the choir, as presently used, an obstacle? Because its *modus operandi* is not only less than fully supportive of congregational singing, but directly in conflict with it. How so? Because:

(a) it requires hymns to be sung at a pitch where the tune is too high for many women and is definitely too high for most men: so that the potential body of sound baulks at the fence of the first high note - and, indeed, most men, through long experience of falling at the fence, are wearily disinclined to attempt the jump.

(b) The symbolism is all too clear: singing is for that lot up there in the chancel, not for the likes of me.

(c) All too often, the accompaniments are based on the harmonies - i.e. the thump thump sequences of chords - rather than on the broad lyrical sweep of the tune, and the rhythmic flow of the words for which the tune is the intended vehicle.

As a result, the congregation's singing of the tune fails to take off.

However, it would be a capital mistake to leave a negative impression in this matter. The purpose must be to liberate, and that must include the liberation of whatever enthusiasm, commitment, talent, and expertise is in the present choir as well as the liberation of these qualities in the congregation and, going beyond the congregation, in the local community at large. And this means breaking through a fear barrier.

Many organists are nervous of their choirs. They have to live with them. They know that there are strong personalities in the choir. They feel - wrongly, in my view, but they feel - that they are dependent on their turning up, Sunday by Sunday, on their putting in extra time for practice, on Sundays, or during the week, on their putting in a lot of extra work for special occasions like Harvest, Christmas, Easter. They depend on their pulling off the anthem on Sunday mornings. And, in many cases, the organist may consider that his professional reputation depends on maintaining the loyalty of the choir, specially if some of its members constitute part of the membership of other musical groups for which he is responsible in the local community.

The minister also is often nervous of the choir. It stands there in full view of the congregation, and if it is not happy, the faces show it. The minister has to handle the organist carefully, keep him or her sweet. Organists do not grow on trees. If this one should leave, where will a replacement come from? From the perspective of the minister, the organ and choir seem to go together, as a vital partnership which must be humoured. All that, however, still sounds negative. Putting it positively, minister, organist and choir share the leadership of worship; so, rather than describing them as nervous, one should say that a good minister will be sensitive to the organist, a good organist sensitive to the choir, and a good choir sensitive to both of them and to the needs of the congregation. In any case, to be fair to the choir, the boot is not infrequently on the other foot: loyal choir members may turn out week after week, when there are a hundred other things they might prefer to be doing, to support an organist who is musically indifferent and personally unsympathetic, and a minister or priest who has no interest in or concern for their musical effort: who not once in a year, for example, comes to the choir after the service and says, "That anthem was terrific - thank you very much indeed for the lift it gave to me and to the whole service."

Before I proceed to some practical conclusions, which I hope will strike a positive note, there are three further remarks about the choir that need to be made, to confirm that I wish not to bury but to praise the church choir, even as presently constituted.

The first is that, whatever its poker-faced or pious image as it sits, gowned or otherwise, but certainly handbagged and pepperminted, its members are frequently lovely people and great fun to work with. Some of the most amusing and rewarding hours of my life have been spent with choirs. Second, they are public performers, as are organists and ministers; and those who have never had to perform anything more arduous in church than the pressing of a reluctant coin into an offertory bag have probably very little understanding of the extra emotional pressure that performing involves. Third, we owe these traditional choirs a huge debt, for during the difficult years of transition from the old world to the new, they have held the fort, keeping musical standards when nobody else cared; helping to create an atmosphere of worship when little else, in sometimes plain church buildings, did; and providing a real shot in the arm when the great festivals of Christmas and Easter came around.

Their function has been inspirational and educational. Church music might not have survived without them. But now we are entering a different era.

In that assessment of the church choir, I have tried to be fair and truthful all round. The first step in any serious review of church music in each local situation will have to be some kind of dialogue, trialogue, or general conversation along such lines; which is why the fear barrier will have to be broken; for only if organist and minister are confident enough to lead and participate calmly in such discussion, in choir, kirk session, and congregation, will they be able to steady nerves, assuage hurt feelings, keep tempers cool, and lead all those involved into a free, truthful or hopeful appreciation of what new kinds of musical expression could be achieved.

Let us postulate that we have got these: the atmosphere is constructive. Everyone is interested in opening out the situation. What alternatives might be offered? Before responding to that question, I make one *caveat*. Again and again in these talks I have said there is no universal panacea. Every situation is unique, with its own problems, its own people, instruments and talents, its own history, its own potential.

What I now offer is, therefore, a stall of suggestions, one, none, or some of which might be useful in some situations, at least as a springboard for experiment.

1 Throw away all the previous vocabulary. There is no longer a church choir.

2 Think variety. There are several singing forces.

3 The first singing force is the congregation.

4 Lower the pitch of most items of praise, so that the congregation can make a fist of the tune. This will only happen if the men can sing it so easily that they enjoy doing so.

5 To lead this primary singing force - the people of God in that situation - give a platform to all the other singing and instrumental forces in the church and community. These may include: the Kirk Session, the Boys' Brigade, the Youth Fellowship or Bible Class Banjo and Ukelele Co-operative, the local comprehensive school jazz band, and the Pub Crawlers and Allied Trades Chauvinist Glee Club.

Is it a coincidence that this list may veer towards the masculine? It is not a coincidence. It is the absence of the male voice that has deprived our hymn singing, even our psalm singing, of its emotional spine. In my Peterhead parish, although we had a good choir and a superb organist, it was on four Sunday mornings in the year that the singing took off: namely at the quarterly communions. And why? The kirk session occupied the choir stalls. As it happened, it was an all-male kirk session. If I had said to them, "You are the choir", they might have become self-conscious, opened their mouths at the appropriate junctures, and emitted demure squeaks and mutters. As it was, forty good men and true allowed their diaphragms to move into flexitime and their larynxes to let rip.

6 Variety being the spice of life, it is not necessary or desirable for every item of praise to have this 'Covenanters marching' quality. There can still be a place for a 'Harmony Choir', that is, the church choir as is now, with a special role to sing anthems, demonstrate new hymns, or occasionally sing a more extended work. And, of course, if that choir is willing to perform also the mundane task of leading the congregational sound by singing mainly in unison, that will be splendid. But variety doesn't stop there. The children's choir, the Sunday School choir, the local school choir, drama group, dance formation; there is no end to the potential variety, so long as the spine remains strong: a comfortable and enjoyable congregational noise which includes in a natural way the men.

7 Variety again. It is not necessary to have five congregational singings. Have, one Sunday, only two - then they are a treat.

Nor is it necessary to stand for all five. Nor need all five be accompanied by the organ. A piano, with a trumpet descant by a local bugle player, will freshen up any old hymn. Nor is it necessary to have any accompaniment. The General Assembly manages fine without it.

8 Speeds. Try hymns which are usually slow, fast. And *vice versa*. Do not, of course, pursue this into the realm of obvious perversity. All I'm talking about is a fresh look. For example, there is a general tendency to take children's hymns at a trot. This dismissive approach seems to stem from no philosphy deeper than small notes for small people. The very simplicity of many children's hymns may be enhanced by the dignity of a steady pace. More important, very young children take time to wrap their brains and tongues around even quite simple words. And sometimes these simple words carry a depth-charge of meaning, which given space, can explode potent parabolic implications.

9 Loudness. The same principle of unpredictable variety applies. The killing thing is an ear-deadening sameness of volume. A very quiet treatment can be as dramatic as a very loud one.

10 In an article I wrote for Life and Work, I said: can we recapture a music grand enough for God? My last suggestion is this: grandeur does not require frills, sophistication or original-ity. A football crowd singing 'Abide With Me' is not sophisti-cated. It may not have all the hallmarks of a sacramental liturgy. But in its emotional freedom it may have something to remind us of - that plain singing from the heart is, even in the context of a cosmos as grand as the one we pass fleetingly through, difficult to match.

In the matter of introducing flexibility and variety of treat-ment, the class leader in Scotland in the last decade has been John Bell. I see him as an ice-breaker. You may recall the whales that were trapped under the rapidly forming ice up there in Alaska. And you will recall the technique used to prepare a path through the ice to the ocean? A series of holes was drilled to enable the surviving whales to breathe as they swam to freedom. Each of John Bell's initiatives - his own hymns and songs, his Iona patterns of worship, his Wild Goose choir and its recordings, and his live liturgical workshops all over Scotland - all this, put together, amounts to a considerable work of liberation. If you see the Scottish church music situation of fifteen years ago as a stranded whale, trapped behind the hardening ice of secular indifference, youthful boredom, and commercial music marketing, what John, Graham Maule, and their Iona partners have been doing is to keep a passage open for Christian worship to survive in a natural singing form.

As someone who in an earlier incarnation had something to do with the music on Iona, I feel confident in saying that to these innovators and custodians of the flame, we all owe a large debt. I add only one caution. If we owe to John and other innovators our support, we owe them also something else: an openness to all styles and traditions. It is not necessary, in accepting the contemporary offerings, to reject the corpus of material that has come down to the people of Scotland from past centuries.

Throughout these reflections, I have recalled illuminating experiences in the company of that most sardonic and least predictable of master conductors, Tommy Beecham. Thirty years ago, I heard him ask in a public lecture, "What, in the last resort, is the purpose of music?" He answered his own rhetorical question. "It is to enable heart to speak to heart." No sardonic overtone, there. He said it from the heart, because he was defending music he loved but knew to be vulnerable - the music of Delius.

An article on Cardinal Newman in The Independent of 24th November 1990 concludes as follows:
"Perhaps thought is music." Newman wrote this not long after completing 'The Dream of Gerontius'. An undergraduate

poem of his had contained the lines,

> There is a spirit singing aye in air
>
> That lifts us high above each mortal care.

- an idea not far from Edward Elgar's idea "that there is music in the air, music all around us". Newman's motto as cardinal, *Cor ad cor loquitur* (heart speaks to heart), seems almost an echo from his mighty Beethoven, who wrote on the score of the 'Missa Solemnis': "From the heart, may it again reach the heart."

In this book I have reminisced about many musicians, and specially organists, teachers, and above all conductors, who reached my heart. Conductors, because they strike chords in my imagination: chords of analogy; because God, if He exists, must have some of the characteristics of a conductor facing an orchestra; much depends on the conductor's sensitive grasp of the creative possibilities of the individuals before him, but without their willing co-operation he is powerless.

My last conductor reminiscence is about a man most of you won't have heard of. His never was a great name, and now he is forgotten. He was a displaced person, a Central European refugee, victim of the Hitler Reich. Karl Rankl became the first post-war music director at Covent Garden Opera. He began to build it up but received more brickbats than bouquets. He followed Walter Susskind as only the second conductor of the permanent S.N.O. (now the Royal Scottish National Orchestra), and while Susskind with his Slavonic flair had sometimes skated over difficult inner details to sweep the orchestra into sparkling surface displays of the romantic repertoire, Rankl began to train the orchestra in its inner parts and in the inner nitty-gritty of the great classics. This made him popular with neither players nor audiences. It any case, unlike the glamorous Susskind, Rankl was an unprepossessing man, with a small angular body in a perpetual state of agitation. Unruly in self-presentation, he was untidy in conducting, with a curious vertical sawing motion of a small baton which described none of the balletic curves of more telegenic arm-wavers. And this agitated style produced untidy playing. Chords were not always together, and indeed, the ensemble could be positively ragged.

Why, then, am I devoting time to him? Because he so often let the cat out of the bag - or, to put it more elegantly, he let the composer out of the cage of history. Especially Beethoven. After over thirty years of hearing Beethoven conducted by great conductors, I would still, on entering Heaven, ask if by any chance Karl Rankl was somewhere down the road, conducting a fifth rate band in a Beethoven Symphony. Why? You heard the inner parts. More than that, you heard the inner parts fighting each other. His Beethoven, entrails displayed, was the equivalent of W.O. Minay's Bach. Both prefigured the deconstructionist architecture exemplified in Lloyd's building in London and in so many of the Olympic buildings in Barcelona, where those parts that enable a building to live and breathe, instead of being concealed, are revealed with a shout. Rankl's agitation went to the heart of Beethoven's agitation. Suffering was revealed. The crucifixion that all human living involves is not resolved by surface ensemble. In a Rankl performance, when the final resolution came, the apotheosis meant something. The heart spoke out of its wounds.

But my definitive memory of Karl Rankl's Beethoven goes back beyond those S.N.O. years. I only once attended a performance of Beethoven's opera 'Fidelio'. It was in those early post-war years, and Covent Garden, doing a provincial tour, came to the King's Theatre, Edinburgh. I guess it was a pretty dowdy production and I remember the Scotsman music critic being lofty about it. I was spellbound. Rankl was, I'm sure, at one with Beethoven in an inner perception of the black chaos that threatens the order of all human personality as well as of society and the world, but also, I suspect, he was existentially at one with Beethoven in an awareness of the eternal temptation to shut up the force of the human spirit in the dungeons of the subconscious, or the dungeons of human institutions, doctrines, rules and conventions, not to mention the physical dungeons of Gulags, concentration camps, torture chambers, gas chambers. Therefore, when in 'Fidelio' the prisoners came out of the dark, blinking in the light, singing their chorus, I received via Beethoven, Karl Rankl, and that undistinguished orchestra and cast, an image of what real human resurrection involves.

That remains for me a key to life, for it reveals what true freedom is worth - which is everything. I have described a recent visit to Prague, still exploring its new and fragile freedom. As the Iron Curtain was dismantled in front of our eyes in recent times, it was that moment in 'Fidelio', grasped in the King's Theatre, Edinburgh, forty or more years ago that repeatedly came into my head. How undiscriminating! Karl Rankl, what an unsatisfactory, untidy conductor you were! And you, Beethoven, what an unoperatic composer you were. Just as well you only wrote the one. Like you couldn't write fugues and you could not write for the human voice. What a musical failure! So why do you matter so much? The point I am making, of course, is that, just as life is untidy and great art is untidy, because neither fits into neat rules, so church life is untidy (which is why I never believed that a smoothly conducted ecumenical movement producing a tidy ecclesiastical ensemble was a particularly enticing offer - for whatever unity means it is only relevant to the human heart if it reaches deep into the agitation and complexity of real life reflected in chaotic freedom redeemed in great art).

Church music, therefore, is not about being tidy. 'Songs of Praise' is a well-tuned entertainment, and can be inspirational television, but well-drilled congregational singing is not what real worship is about. The question is: what is going on in public worship? If it is something real, then a 'standard' - which so often means a standardisation - of musical performance is not the name of the game. The game begins where I have said it begins, and its name is: the *Logos*, the Word. In the beginning, which. In the beginning, wherefrom. In the beginning, whereof.

I have never believed, myself, that Roman Catholicism should be allowed to claim the implications of transubstantiation as its prerogative. It is one of the pleasant ironies of the dance of evolution that just as Romans are getting apologetically twitchy about such concepts, explaining them away as linguistic formulations, heavily endowed with Italianate rhetorical floridity, medieval philosophical categories, obsolete Newtonian physics, and a discredited Tridentine liturgical approach to the Mass, we R.C.s, as George MacLeod used to describe Reformed Catholics, are moving more openly into the Age of Aquarius, where alchemy is about to be rediscovered in new art, new cosmology and physics, and new discoveries about the body-mind relationship. I have always felt, through a wide diversity of liturgical experience, that worship is about more than individual therapy, social celebration, or community recharging of ethical and political batteries. These are all admirable, but do they justify the ultimate lunacy of baying at the moon, of singing hymns to a being or beings or force fields in other dimensions? So what is going on? The Word, the *Logos*, is going on. It is becoming flesh, it is incarnate, it speaks, it goes through the arc of Christmas, Good Friday, Easter. My Free Church forbears understood this. They did not edit out Christmas and Easter. They celebrated both every Sunday.

If you look closely even at an apparently music-led man like John Bell, you find he is led by the Word. For him too, in the beginning was, and is, the Word. His sparky, feisty tunes and sometimes his austere and tender tunes, speak to my feet, my sense of rhythm, my psyche, my brain, and sometimes my heart. But it is his words which reach from his soul to mine. If you look up Number 11 in 'Songs of God's People', you will see a great hymn by John and Graham Maule, based on John 1. It says what has to be said about the Incarnation.

> Before the world began one word was there;
> grounded in God he was, rooted in care;
> by him all things were made,
> in him was love displayed,
> through him God spoke and said,
> *I am for you.*

Life found in him its source, death found its end;
light found in him its course, darkness its friend;
for neither death nor doubt
nor darkness can put out
the glow of God, the shout:
I am for you.

The Word was in the world which from him came;
unrecognised he was, unknown by name;
one with all humankind,
with the unloved aligned,
convincing sight and mind:
I am for you.

© Wild Goose Publications 1987
Pearce Institute, Glasgow

John's own tune is not quite strong enough to match those words. He has time to find one.

But Incarnation, the central theme of Iona in the post-MacLeod phase, is not the end of the story. The Word, having become Flesh, became torn. The Platonic ideal, perfect in form, became untidy. Chaos resumed its free path, dissolving human attempts at order, even sanctified new order. But the *Logos* was not dead, is not dead. Within the divine nut is the kernel. Beneath the hard winter is the seed of the rose. Under the ice, the corn, the cherry blossom, the apple which inspired Solomon's song of love, they all have a future. So do we. At Easter, children still roll eggs. The origin of the act is mostly forgotten, but we can, by an effort, remember that what gives any worship its *raison d'être*, amid all its daft and feeble compromises, is that the tomb, the unhatching egg of death, gave new birth to us all, and wings for the future to fly.

I described my music master of forty years ago, Tommy Evans. He said one day, "I am going to lay a rather large egg." He did. He extracted it from the reluctant jaws of four hundred rugby playing schoolboys and it hatched into two riotous operas - 'The Bartered Bride', that national opera of the Czech people, of whom I have spoken as a symbol of resurrection, and 'Der Freischutz', that early romantic flower from the Central European seedbed of belief in a magic which can alchemise human disorder, redeem human disaster, and even enable Europe - and Israel - to survive the Holocaust. If religious magic cannot do such things, it is not magic, not even useful myth, merely a very thin gilt on an exceedingly crumbly gingerbread.

I concluded my remarks about this modest musician and teacher by saying that Tommy Evans introduced me to music as fun, so that neither then nor since would worship and fun seem in my mind to be separate.

If the resurrection is a false hope, then that discovery, though wonderful, is ultimately unconsoling. But if, as I believe, resurrection in our time, in our place, and in our lives, is the one thing of which we can be certain, then even in our own local worship there is absolutely everything to play for. Each of us is free to lay our egg. We cannot foretell how or what it will hatch. But if we are truly open, then out of whatever transitional untidy chaos, a form will emerge, and, if we care enough, or even if we don't, I think God will be in it.

Or, if you find that too emphatic, let us earthbound people who are but beginners in cosmic arts and liturgies put in 'L' for learner and call it Gold. Gold will be in it.

EPILOGUES

1 BLESSED ASSURANCE

What? A prologue... the book... now epilogues? In the interval between delivering the lectures and revising them for publication, inevitably I have entertained further reflections. So I have set myself the final task of bringing together a few threads. What follows are my end thoughts: my summary to myself of what all this has been about.

What it was about, essentially, was reassurance. I wanted to reassure... well, just about everyone. My experience is that pessimism, anxiety, and low expectations are bad for work. People do best when they are relaxed and hopeful. Complacency and slackness do not, of course, produce good work, but the right kind of creative tension will normally exert its benign pressure most effectively when the background is optimistically supportive. The church management responsible for worship - in effect, clergy and organists - seem to be on the defensive. They have, on the face of it, some reason to be, because the proliferation of untraditional music and new forms of worship, now championed by the new Archbishop of Canterbury, is often accompanied by a barrage of criticism of traditional forms.

Organists and clergy need reassuring, therefore, that what they have devoted their lives and talents to is not to be despised, apologised for, or cravenly retreated from. But that is the least of it. More than that, they could do with being told that what they offer is inspirational, that it is needed, that it is wanted. If they know this, the upside is that they may step out of their bunker and feel in a strong enough position to be open to new ideas. For the one thing which holds out no hope in this situation is any kind of stand-off. Where rigid positions are adopted, talent is wasted, congregations and communities disrupted, and worship diminished.

Congregations also need encouragement. They need to know that singing is not an achievement orientated challenge, an outward bound obstacle course, a competition, an exam. It is for enjoyment; and they, too, need to know that they are needed. They are going to respond the more freely if they sense that experts are not meting out judgements on their 'standards' of taste or of musical accomplishment. Much of what I had to say was, in fact, about something which should be second nature to at least Reformed church people: democracy.

But there again, there is a benign side-effect. If the people in the pew feel appreciated; relished rather than tolerated, then they will be more open to the specialist roles of the leaders: organist, choir, and clergy.

The hidden, or not so hidden, agenda in all this is excellence. The pursuit of excellence is where intentions of goodwill so often founder. *Gloria in Excelsis* is not about heights of musical discrimination or technique, but neither is it about spatial geography. It is, in some sense, about getting high. In the experience of rising, or being raised above the mundane (and if music is not about that, what on earth is it about?), there has to be an exchange between freedom (democracy) and truth (excellence). In that transaction, neither should lose out entirely, though many differing shades of compromise will transpire in different local situations. To make any of this happen everyone must be prepared to take risks, massive ones if necessary, and everyone must be ready to be tolerant, massively so if necessary. The trick here is basic: it is to permit a comfortable ambiguity in the definition of values. Take excellence and truth, for example. It was in an attempt to introduce flexibility into such definitions that I sat at the piano each evening after the formal lecture and, skating lightly over matters musical and hymnological, tried to show how traditional material can be treated in a variety of ways. What follows now is a kind of graph which describes the outline, but cannot reproduce the essence, of that keyboard operation. Being a graph only, it is no way a transcript of the words used or the notes played.

I have always resisted emotional blackmail, from whatever quarter it comes. In the area of hymns (which I identified as the practical fulcrum of most church music) it works out like this: I reject any pressure to believe that musical and verbal material between 1500 and 1900 is less relevant to present and future needs, than material from (say) 1950 to 1990. Even if the music of the last forty years was, in comparison with the music of the last four centuries, beyond peradventure brilliantly and uniquely perspicacious, I would doubt that, in relation to the vistas of the future, it should be granted a specially authorised spiritual visa. Since I am sure that the opposite is the case, then one of my objectives has to be that hungry souls and minds have access to all that these last four centuries have bequeathed us - including that century known as Victorian. Whatever you've got, whatever the material, new or old, and whatever your musical resources, accept and use it.

2 CHOOSING THE INSTRUMENT

As I sat there at the beautiful piano in the Hutcheson Hall, I was in my mind addressing a few thousand organists round Scotland. Not brilliant organists, not trained choirmasters most of them, but men and women who care.

And what I wanted to say to all of them was something like this. Alright, you may not have a fantastic instrument. You yourself may not be, technically speaking, a prodigious player. Your church is not Westminster Abbey or even St. Giles. But do not underestimate the cards you have to play. After all, you have a remarkable brute of an angel at your command. If it is an even halfway decent pipe organ, you are on Cloud Nine, or should be. Here is a transcendental vehicle for your imagination. All these pipes. This (relatively) vast acoustic chamber for them to resonate in. Plus the marvels of modern electronic gadgetry to enable them to do exactly what you want them to, exactly when.

If it is not a pipe organ, it is probably an electronic organ of some kind. That's not bad. Divine creation works through the ingenuity of human brain and hand, and these have been at work with the musical microchip. There is now a wide range of keyboards and organs which, though they cannot compete in acoustic performance with real pipes in real space, are streets ahead of the basic electronic organ of thirty years ago, with its imitation cinema organ tone (the true cinema organ of half a century ago had genuine grandeur). Not all electronic devices give you the range of a fullblown computer organ, and not all synthesisers have laser beams à la Jean Michel Jarre, but even the meanest Yamaha can produce sounds which, when experimented with, can be fun, even, if imaginatively used, evocative. The key here is not to pretend they are conventional pipe organs. Don't blatter out loud organ-like sounds. Not for long, anyway.

When organs, even electronic ones, fail, or fail to materialise, you can count your lucky stars. This may be just the opportunity your colleagues in other churches, stuck with indifferent instruments, would give their eye-teeth for. Now you have a copper-bottomed excuse for experimenting, which should be seized with both hands.

First port of call will be a piano. If a grand, or baby grand is available, you're in clover. This can provide an exciting variety of mood, style, and support for much, or most, of what is needed. But first things first. Is it in tune? Not just vaguely, or almost, in tune, but really, with no sourness. Is it producing a full rounded tone, not only in the middle, but top and bottom? If not, it is worth a great deal of effort to acquire the services of a reputable tuner. Piano tuning is not the busy trade it once was. Craftsmen and women in this field are scarce. But do not, on that account, settle lazily for an amateur, or even someone like a piano teacher round the corner who sometimes tunes parlour uprights on the side. If a good piano is going to be the basis for your music then it deserves, and needs, as serious attention as a pipe organ. If you live within reach of a major city, there should be someone who, by appointment, with all expenses paid, would be willing to come. That might even apply, at longer notice, to a piano in a rural community. To get professional advice about reputable tuners, approach professional musical organisations who need reliable piano tuning for public concerts. I lay stress on this because I am sure the potential of a good piano is radically underestimated by bodies like Kirk Sessions. We're almost certainly not talking about a concert grand. A church able to afford that scale of investment would be more likely to look for a pipe organ or a classy synthesiser system. But there are various sizes of non-uprights, down to the boudoir instrument. It's a matter of looking around and being realistic about the acoustics of the building involved. A resonant building can add a surprising roundness of tone to a modest piano - but the tone has to have some quality in the first place or what the building will magnify will be harshness, tinniness, or strings inaccurately tuned.

Having got your piano, then enjoy it. Few things are more frustrating than hearing hymns played 'correctly' on a piano; played from the page in correct chord formation, with as much tonal and rhythmic reinforcement as a scotch trifle has sherry. Traditional organists (and pianists) can perhaps learn something from the evangelical tradition, with its partly American negro roots and its Moody and Sankey colouring. But, if rhythm and blues, soul, or jazz alienate you, or leave you cold, we have our British traditions: the Salvation Army, the Baptist, Methodist, and other non-conformist influences, and the host of new styles which have sprung up in recent years. You don't have to go along with all their music or words to appreciate the freedom with which these traditions treat the keyboard. In fact, it is worth issuing a caution here: acquiring a piano is not going automatically down market. Just because it is a piano, not an organ, that lies under your hands does not mean you have to go looking mainly in 'new' music or in songs written pianistically for voice and keyboard. The full tonal range of the piano can be just as effective when deployed to turn a classic psalm or hymn into a full-bodied concerto for congregation and piano. Use all the devices a piano can offer - octaves in bass and treble, the use of organ-like sostenuto tone, and the rhythmic edge offered by the percussive capacity of the piano. And equally, the full range of bass and treble, when played quietly, can have a crystallinely magic effect in a resonant building.

But what of the truly dire situation, where no such instrument is available? What you have is a boring old upright piano! Is this where you resign, either actually from the job of leading the music, or inwardly to weekly defeat at the hands, so to speak, of an unspeakable honky-tonk? No way. Here is your greatest opportunity. Possibly the best worship programme we transmitted on Radio Scotland in my seventeen years in the BBC, was from Priesthill Primary School in a run-down deprived housing

estate in Glasgow. It certainly was one of the programmes which
had the most impact. Pat Walker, then Head of Programmes,
BBC Scotland, reported that it galvanised his household, and they
would have been happy to hear it all straight through again at
once. The impact derived mainly from the music. Which was? A
honky-tonk. Squashed into a corner of the small hall was this
grotesquely ungracious apology for a piano. No, that is precisely
the wrong word. The last thing, it, or anyone else, did was to
apologise. Round this primitive machine was assembled as *ad hoc*
a collection of scratch performers as could be imagined out of a
street busker's nightmare. A drum here, a triangle there, and was
there a skiffle bass, a castanet, a clarinet? To be honest, I don't
remember. It didn't matter. What mattered was two things: the
infection of the rhythm, and the tornado of vocal response from
the school. I'm not sure if it was singing or shouting; occasionally
it was almost screaming, but it was - it really was, I swear - great
music-making. The genius who alchemised these unlikely resources into a paean of praise wasn't even a music teacher. Just a
teacher with a gift for communication and an uninhibited reaction to an upright piano. Yes, he thumped, rather than cajoled it.
But with love. And Donald Macdonald, the producer, liberated
the love.

That is almost enough said, perhaps, about pianos, and about
using whatever resources are locally available; but there is one
more point to be made, arising out of the emotional blackmail
factor I mentioned at the beginning of this section. There is no
need to be caught between the devil of modernity and the deep
(blue) sea of tradition. Duck out of the crossfire between those
who would think a piano, even a good one, was a secular
excrescence, and those who would think a piano, specially a good
one, a fuddy-duddy relic of the 19th Century middle-class addiction to Chopin. Each of those notions is as silly as the other.

The piano, shorn of its parlour image, is the most versatile
and classy musical instrument ever invented, and capable of an
almost infinite flexibility of mood. That is why it carried the
romantic tradition of Chopin and Rachmaninov into the mid-
20th Century piano playing of George Shearing and Dave
Brubeck. And that is why it sustained the art of song over the last
couple of centuries, not only in the *lieder* tradition of Schubert,

but in the Cole Porter, Gershwin, Irving Berlin *lieder* traditions of this century. More surprising, perhaps, to those who assume that the songs of our time were trapped between loud bands and electronic back-up groups on the one hand and the strummings of guitars on the other, the piano has continued to provide the mainstay for many of the great ballads of the hit stars of the Seventies and Eighties.

I'm not suggesting that the piano is the ideal solution for most church music problems. I'm just saying its value is unnecessarily underestimated. So whose side am I on? The brilliant classical organist's or the *ad hoc* pub-pianist's? Neither, and both. I'm on everybody's side who cares and throws himself or herself off the cliff of opportunity presented by Barth's "state of affairs". As I tried to describe it in the lectures, this implies that if we accept the raw material of our actual situation, and place that truthfully in the hands of God, there is, in the dimension of Christ's redemption, scarcely any limit to the creative use to which that raw material may be put.

Anyone who has heard Donald Swann sing one of his epic serious songs to his own accompaniment will have heard the piano erupt into such multi-dimensional tones as to make an organ or orchestra sound like a fairground noise.

3 RUMMAGING AMONG THE TUNES

If free enjoyment of whatever instrument or combination of instruments is available is a *sine qua non*, hardly less so is free enjoyment of whatever material is available for singing. Material for choral or instrumental ensemble is outside the scope of these lectures. Apart from the fact that it is a specialist area, one of my main conclusions is that the key to a church music revival lies in congregational singing. Since my whole aim is to make things easy, comfortable, unintimidating and improveable without undue hassle in the here and now, my basic suggestion has to be easy: and it is. Whatever the congregation uses is fine. In the Church of Scotland, it is probably CH3, very possibly supplemented by Songs for God's People, and at Christmas time by sheets of carols. Whether supplied only with the first, or with all three, what you have there is a treasure chest. All you have to do is fling open the lid, dig in both hands, and enjoy a good rummage. Methodists, Congregationalists (or United Reformed), Anglicans, and others, have equally good, or better books.

In a couple of my piano sessions at the end of the lectures, I enjoyed a few digs at CH3. Because, like Mount Everest, it is there. In particular, I confessed more than mild surprise at some of the omissions. All anthologies leave things out. What activated my critique (so to dignify a number of loosely connected examples) was the suspicion that there was in the editorial mind a conscious or unconscious disengagement from (that sounds more polite than vendetta against) Victoriana. I demonstrated at the piano, to at least my satisfaction, that the 'old' tunes for 'Fight the Good Fight', 'Lead Kindly Light', and 'Make Me a Captive, Lord', were capable of a sustained smouldering passion that 'Duke Street', 'Ich Halte Treulich Still', and 'Lux Benigna' all fine tunes, were simply not built for. 'Duke Street' and 'Ich Halte Treulich Still', in particular, are too good, in a way too vigorous. Too good, too vigorous? Surely this is nonsense. I quoted in Chapter One the Chairman of Courtaulds saying that the best is the enemy of the good. 'Duke Street' is a great tune, which leaps about athletically, swiping here, there, and everywhere, knocking out all comers and climaxing with élan. But I heard my one-armed organist Tom Galloway play 'Fight the Good Fight' when his remaining arm was riddled with cancer. The 'old' tune 'Pentecost' burned and crunched with a sense of profound inner struggle, not a *macho* display of prowess. In parenthesis, it is ludicrous, is it not, to call them old tunes. Medieval? 18th Century? They were written at the height of the British Empire, the time when Glasgow's industry dominated the world, and theology was explosively dominating Scotland's intellectual scene. And the 'old' hymnbook, the Revised Church Hymnary, was, after all, a 20th Century publication.

I underline this obvious point to reaffirm that value judgements based on the sliced loaf approach to history are worthless, and to encourage those who believe in 'old' tunes to feel free to reintroduce them, despite their absence from one particular slice of the loaf called CH3. The more general deduction to be made is that the editorial decisions of one transitory hymn-book (soon, no doubt, to be superseded) do not evince the authority of even a *scintilla* of holy writ. Nevertheless, CH3 is, as I said, despite its limitations, a treasure chest, so let it be freely plundered. Let it be pragmatically plundered. Ignore its cavilling restrictions, fly lightly over its fences of editorial jurisdiction. For example, it is beyond me to understand on what theological, pastoral, historical, musicological, liturgical-historical, tragical-pastoral, or any other comical basis the editors split Advent in two: the First Coming and, half a hymnbook later, the Second Coming. Irritating though that is, one just ignores it. But when it comes to choice of tunes, ignoring is not what one should do. For example, 'Hark the Glad Sound' is set to 'Bristol'. Now 'Bristol' is a fine dignified tune, none better. It proceeds majestically across country with the measured tread of a theological earth-mover. It is not, however, designed for flying. But 'Crediton' (the 'old' tune) is designed for flying. It gets off the ground and, once off, it stays there.

Look at verse one. "Hark" is meant to alert you, like a fire alarm. The once-off dotted rhythm for verse one does just that. Never mind that half the congregation miss it. If they're that dozy, they deserve to. But it will prime their batteries.

And look at verse five. "Heaven's Arches Ring". That is where 'Crediton' gratifyingly loops the loop. Whereas, at that point, Bristol is pawing the ground and asking, "Heaven? Where's that?" It was crazy to divorce 'Crediton' from that paraphrase. Only a Hollywood New York lawyer could have so enthusiastically scissored an excellent match. Whereas, lo and behold, 'Bristol' is absolutely perfect for Hymn 162 in CH3, which was given 'Crediton'. And 'Neumark', attached by CH3 to 162, is perfect for 163, where its dignity matches John 1 hand to glove.

I'm not saying I'm right and CH3 is wrong. I'm saying, everyone is fallible. Don't be overawed by editorial decisions. Don't believe everything you read in print - even this. Make your own assessments. Then decide freely. Be your own man or woman. If you're a clergyperson, feel free to say to the musician, "Hey, what about doing this?" If you're the musician, feel absolutely free to say to the pulpitperson, "Ah, look, don't you see, this goes so much better with that?"

I'm sure all this is unnecessary. You're doing it already? Well then, I'm applauding.

4 LOUDNESS, PITCH AND SPEED

Now I come into a really dodgy area. It's dodgy because in this matter nearly everyone I'm potentially talking to will think they know more about it than me. The two subjects are speed and pitch. In cricket, these two things come together. In hymns, scarcely less so.

There is no way that in print I can portray what one could at the piano. So I am reduced (or expanded) to porridge-like pronouncements, complete with indigestible lumps.

On speeds: be your own person. THINK. I mean, think from scratch. Think, each Sunday. Assumptions I would challenge include the following:

Big congregations sing slow. Small groups sing fast.
Psalms are slow. Marching hymns are fast. Reflective hymns are slow. Hymns of positive praise are fast.
Good Friday is slow. Easter Sunday is fast.

And so on. In other words, throw the packaged stereotypes overboard.

Yes, often a psalm is best sung slow. Indeed, let me call your bluff over this assumption. Have you ever tried it really slow? I mean, really, really. I have, to the point that the congregation simply couldn't believe it, and verse one sank like the Titanic. But then, gradually, the penny dropped and the Titanic rose. By the last verse, the icebergs were scattered, and there was a momentous sound, as words sung by the Covenanters sailed to their inexorable conclusion.

But equally, you can double the speed for a lively psalm. So long as you accompany lightly, with the organ pedal working only the first beat of the bar (or, on occasion, of every second bar), there need be no sense of fuss or harassment. Even a large congregation will grasp the intention and become fleet of foot.

The same, of course, applies to hymns. On the morning that I took the psalm very slowly, I took the next item, 'Praise to the

Lord' ('Lobe den Herren') very fast. It is, after all, a waltz, and I made it a quick one. I think it worked.

This pragmatic approach works right across the board. I referred in Chapter Seven to children's hymns. It is insulting to assume that they should be always fast. Take a modern classic, which has become almost a Sunday School anthem: Sydney Carter's 'The Lord of the Dance'. I have the advantage of having heard Sydney sing this. He does so, as he sings all his songs, with a kind of rhythm which is neither fast nor slow, but always immensely poised. The source of this poise is the stringent attention he is paying to the words. The words, after all, are his. He takes them seriously. To him, they are as theological as anyone's Dogmatics. Incidentally, when did you last give these particular words a good read? I would dare you to do that and then go into church and race through the tune. The tune doesn't, in any case, invite a sprint. Listen to Aaron Copland's 'Appalachian Spring' and hear the tune given a wonderfully taut and elegant space.

In the beginning was the Word. Yes, always. I won't repeat all that I said in Chapter Seven about the possibilities latent in being very pragmatic indeed about pitch. Let me only report that at the end of that final lecture, I invited the audience to try to sing various hymns at high and low pitches, and fast and slow speeds, and asked them then to vote on the various treatments. I see no reason why this democratic procedure should not be adopted in congregational singing. That doesn't mean that any particular vote has to be conclusive. If the musician has strong views on what might work, let him or her come back again and again and experiment, demonstrate, propose.

It intrigued me, on this occasion, as I noted in the Prologue, that views on pitch appeared to split right down the middle. On one side were organists and choir members from churches where everything seemed to be hunky-dory. They were outraged at the suggestion that the pitch might be radically lowered. On the other side were people from the pews, plus one or two organists where everything was far from fine, who agreed strongly that the pitch needed to be drastically lowered to accommodate, as I had argued, the average voice, as distinct from the ideal male and female larynx.

Again, however, I am not seeking to lay down a new convention, merely to urge freedom to try out anything which might play a part in liberating the voice of the people. Take loudness, for example. It simply isn't the case that loudness is always exciting and quietness always dull. Think of the last time you attended a performance of one of the great choral classics - Messiah, Gerontius, any of the famous Requiems or Masses. Which was the most thrilling moment? Yes, it may well have been one of the towering climaxes. But think again, which was the second most thrilling moment? Was it not when the huge forces assembled there sank into a deep pianissimo that can really make the hairs on the back of the neck prickle. There is no reason why a congregation, large or small, should not sing quietly. I've heard it happen at Christmas services when a large congregation, allowed to sit for some of the carols, feels comfortable enough to sing in a relaxed way which produces a wonderfully rounded and unforced tone. In my Peterhead parish, at the Watchnight Service, I sometimes encouraged people to hum certain verses. Even without a solo voice soaring over it, that could be magical. Why should such simple devices be tried only at Christmas? It's nice to have that annual amnesty from the obligation to stand up five times in a service, square the shoulders, stick out the chest, clear the throat, and... squawk; but why not let people sit more often for a reflective or, as it used to be called, a devotional hymn or song? It is perfectly respectable. No discourtesy to the deity is implied. Free Church congregations, by no means liturgical hooligans, sit as they sing the psalms, and so do our Reformed brethren on the Continent.

But, at the risk of flogging a restive if not dead horse, it must be pointed out that if it is difficult for most men and many women to sing loudly at the pitch of most hymns, it is virtually impossible for them to sing top notes quietly unless that pitch is decisively lowered.

I'm not biased against the great climactic shout. Far from it. The Priesthill primary school I quoted is a shining example to us all of what liberated psyches may accomplish. And I have pitched in, so to speak, with the best of them, as an enthusiastic member of muscularly Christian congregations singing their liberated heads off in Fettes College Chapel or St. Giles Cathedral. But liberation is the word. I referred in Chapter Two to the common-sense doctrine of Sir Adrian Boult about an architectural perspective on climaxes - one main one, the rest scaled from that. If congregations are offered light and shade, and if every singing is not a muscular chore, then when a big climax comes they are the more likely to be willing and able to take off. Always, there has to be proportion. If the service goes in the opposite direction and droops through a succession of dull boring items, drained of energy, then the congregation's lungs and spirits will terminally droop, and the bit climax will never happen. Singing quietly is not to sing without energy. The most wearying thing of all is monotony, whether quiet or loud.

In all these matters, it is a question of balancing the detail against the whole. At the piano, I gave examples of how certain conductors and organists in Brahms, Mendelssohn, Mozart and Bach, demonstrated that the need to give space to certain details of phrasing dictated the overall speed. I then analogously played certain hymn and psalm tunes to illustrate how, if particular words and grace notes were to be allowed their verbal and musical space and not to be trivialised by rushing over them, this inevitably led to a more gracious (not slow) speed being adopted than one sometimes hears.

5 MAKING THE OLD NEW

The same general principle applies to the Christian year of worship. Every Sunday need not be, cannot be, a high feast day. This is a tricky matter, theologically, psychologically and musically. Theologically, because, in the Reformed theology of liturgy, the whole cycle of the creation and salvation story is, at least implicitly, enacted each week. Psychologically, because in pastoral terms it is dangerous to play around too much with moods. Who are you, as minister, priest, or musician, to dictate the mood of the individual worshipper? You may, for all kinds of admirable reasons, plan a service which is quiet, reflective, subdued, but someone in a pew who has spent the week sinking into an all-too-quiet labyrinth of self-doubt may need, this

Sunday morning, to be caught up in a wave of confidence as the resilient faith of those around rises in loud affirmation. Conversely, you may plan a lively exciting service, but here in a pew is a person in the toils of depression or bereavement, or just in a valued state of peace, who hoped for a space out of the world's noise and finds all this loud playing and singing jarringly bombastic. Musically, the difficulty is that if you have high days, then the low days may seem just that: low in energy, anti-climactic.

Again, it is a matter of perspective. In my opinion, never should an act of worship lack verbal or musical energy, and never should it be allowed to sag. Episodic worship withers on the vine. The creative tension must describe a span from beginning to end. This applies just as much to 'sad' occasions as cheerful ones, just as much to funerals as to weddings. It even applies to Good Friday. Who benefits from the kind of Good Friday event, especially if it extends over a three hour vigil, which, from a starting point of compulsory solemnity, unravels down descending steps of lachrymose piety into a miasma of gloom?

I'm reminded of the devastating review written by Christopher Grier in his first year as music critic of The Scotsman. He had been to his first Usher Hall 'St. Matthew Passion' by the Edinburgh Bach Choir and he referred disparagingly to a series of "vaguely pious sounds" floating across the hall from the platform. It was a touch cruel, but he made his point. That is a criticism nobody would have levelled at the Herrick Bunney performances of the same work, in their sense of urgency and - yes - passion. Were they any the less pious, in the true sense? Of course not. *Au contraire.*

Just as hymns in general may benefit from a fresh review of their speed, in particular some 'sad' hymns can be rescued from the doldrums by a radical reconsideration of the speed and rhythm. This is especially true of what we know as the German Reformation Chorales. Some of them are arrangements by Bach, adapted by Mendelssohn, but that doesn't make them any more suitable for our congregational use. It is quite impossible for a normal congregation to sustain, let alone impart energy to, hymns like 'Wake, Awake' and 'A Safe Stronghold' at the speed and pitch, and with the harmonic stolidity incorporated in the Revised Church Hymnary and in CH3. This is especially galling when it is known that in their original form, these tunes, and others like them, were energetic, lithe, rhythmic, and fun to sing. It is true that continental congregations still sometimes sing such chorales in the heavy manner, but many others, with astringent new song books, sing the more rhythmic original versions, and in unison. If the truth be known, many of our metrical psalm tunes were similarly metamorphosed. Originally, they were lively enough for an English bishop to refer to them as "these Geneva jigs". But it was Luther who asked why the devil should have the best tunes and it was he, an enthusiastic lute and flute player and composer, who adapted, among other material, contemporary folk songs. Was 'O Sacred Head' not originally a secular love song, with a lilting pulse? Is there any reason why it should not lilt today, even on Good Friday? Or why with different words, it should not throb with urgency?

I have some reason to be happy with the Passion Chorale's attachment to the Chesterton hymn 'O God of Earth and Altar', as I was, I believe, the person who joined them together. Just another instance of a one-off risk becoming institutionalised! History need not dictate to us, one way or another, in those questions of style. But we need to know that we are free to knock the stuffing out of unhelpful traditions and let tunes be re-animated, so that dynamic thoughts can breathe again freely.

So how should we deal with the great German classics? The answer is, in essence, simple. Sing them in unison, with rhythm, sometimes faster, and often lower. If it can be taken, then, that there is no spiritual or musical justification for dullness, greyness, blandness, or somnolence in any kind of service, the way is open, without anxiety, to vary the diet throughout the year, with relative high and low points, relative light and shade, relatively vivid colour contrasting with more subtle toning. And as I said in Chapter Seven, there is no need for every service to have five items of congregational praise. Equally, there is no reason why a whole service should not be geared round community singing (presumably thematically linked) or round a sequence of high quality performances by choir and/or instrumentalists, for sitting and listening is just as much worship as standing and singing, as Anglican cathedral worship recognises in deeply spiritual services such as Choral Evensong.

All the above comments have been directed at having a fresh look at traditional material. What about new material? To go into detail about the increasing amount of recent and contemporary publishing in this field would have required a separate exercise. My main aim has been to reassure people that we can kickstart quite a sufficient musical reformation right now where we are, with the material that is at hand, so that nobody can plead the *alibi* of not knowing this or that technique, or not having this or that resource, or not knowing this or that kind of old or new music. Any minister or musician worth his or her salt is sooner or later going to do research into other sources both old and new, but in the meantime we can begin the new revolution with the old tools, and we can begin next Sunday.

A prominent theme in these reflections has been the supposed tension between old and new. Those who are concerned for the new will think I have been over-concerned for the old. I hope that is not so. My concern has been to preserve the living soil of our ordinary worship, for that is the seed-bed of tomorrow's flowering; and so I would like to renew confidence in everything that has nourished that soil and can continue for the forseeable future. I have questioned the concept of old and new in the context of music. Beauty and truth, I sentimentally believe, are for ever. But 'ever' is not a long straight line, it is a loop through the human and divine spirit. Musical and spiritual freedom involves the privilege of being alive at any time and in any place and to have access to the experiences of others which have been enshrined in any time and place in artifacts, because they still provide the most widespread access in most of our church communities. They are channels which lead to open seas where many a spiritual adventure may still be launched.

I referred in Chapter Two to arriving back from Prague, and finding that Leonard Bernstein had died. A couple of weeks after the last of these lectures, BBC TV broadcast a special edition of 'Omnibus' which paid tribute to Bernstein. Michael Tilson Thomas, one of the finest of the new generation of American conductors, now principal conductor of the London Symphony Orchestra, described the impact of 'Lenny' on himself and other young musicians at Tanglewood, the summer home of the Boston Symphony. He said that before Bernstein arrived, the idea, under composers like Aaron Copland, was to search out new paths. There was the classical path here and the new music path there. Lenny made it "one whole wide path, stretching 360° in possibility, the idea of music as a universal expression of mankind; and the purpose of a life was to explore all of the music, and for one to enrich the other."

That rings true of the composer of 'West Side Story' and the Chichester Psalms. There's a very simple point here. Our sense of historical perspective is not wide enough to separate dross from gold. One Vienna critic said Schubert couldn't write tunes. TUNES? In a different field, planners in the '60s wanted to demolish Gilbert Scott's St. Pancras station in London, as a Victorian monstrosity, a blot on the brave new world of tinted glass rectangles. Now, a mere thirty years later, the race is on to restore it to its former glory. Where yesterday's *kitsch* is today's cult, what will be tomorrow's trend? Better to remain unsnared in these smart debates, and trust your own emotional response.

As a young man, Bernstein became famous overnight when he had to conduct the New York Philharmonic at no notice at all because Bruno Walter had flu. Bruno Walter is one conductor I haven't reminisced about in these pages, but I referred to him in one of the piano sessions. I played 'The Blue Danube' waltz and asked: is this new or old? For a world that is gone or for our world? In answering my question, I recollected the *matinée* concert in the Usher Hall on the last day of the first Edinburgh Festival in 1947. What had made the Festival lift off, by encouraging great artists to participate, was Bruno Walter's agreement to reunite with the Vienna Philharmonic at Edinburgh. Hitler, the Holocaust, the War, had separated them. It was a Viennese concert, and as the marches and polkas crackled and the waltzes glided, I saw from the organ loft the tears in the orchestra and on the face of Lotte Walter, and the conflict between light and shade on Walter's face.

They were in mourning for a world that had passed away. But the bitter-sweetness in the music was integral to it, and so was the emotional aspiration which is at the heart of every age. So, although it was a glorious surprise when in the Stanley Kubrick film '2001' the soundtrack for the first sequence in space was 'The Blue Danube', it did not jar. Music from a past world had leapfrogged over the present and was illuminating future worlds. If a late 20th Century epic of the cinema dealing with 21st Century matters is not too proud to use 19th Century music - music, moreover, for a *passé* social mode - then it is difficult to see why Christian musicians and clergy, following a cult based on events of two to three thousand years ago, should be so fastidious about Victorian hymnody.

Because, unlike the Blue Danube, so many 19th Century hymns are doleful dirges?

On the 4th April 1993, virtually at the time of going to press, the South Bank Show showed a film. If a film can be, this was a dirge. It was slower than any hymn. And sadder. And very much longer than an hour. It consisted of the Polish composer Henryk Gorecki's 3rd Symphony, entitled 'Symphony of Sorrowful Songs'. Tony Palmer's film overlaid on a complete performance of this most uniformly sombre of all 20th Century laments, images of the horrors of our time: Auschwitz, Somalia, Iraq, Sarajevo. Inexorably pressed home by the unrelenting orchestral throb and the soprano's cry of mother for child, child for mother, and all for God, it was all but unbearable. The Samuel Barberesque harmonies were such as would fit any popular hymn. Who could want such stuff? An unprecedented number of people. This symphony has sold more recordings than any classical work written this century, reached number six in the pop chart album last January, and sold over 300,000 compact discs world-wide. Why? It is about death. It confronts death. Everything is stripped from the human heart. Why do we expect the music of our cross-centred faith to do less?

Yes, our faith goes beyond death, and our music has to outrun the dark places of the heart, but if we try to bypass either we bypass the mass of people that music exists to serve.

6 AND LASTLY...

The river of life flows on. Chapter Five opened with my recollection of the 1938 showing of the film 'Sixty Glorious Years', starring Anna Neagle in a pre-war world which bears no relation to ours. A month after delivering that lecture I was transfixed to see on my television set a clip from that ancient film, my first sighting of it for 52 years. What unfixed me, brought me to my feet indeed, was the lively conversation that followed. The presenter was chatting to an attractive dynamic lady whom I had carelessly assumed to have gone long since to wherever stars go when they die. This was Anna Neagle, and she was still performing in front of my eyes. She described how she never thought she would get anywhere because she was always so 'tongue-tied and stupid' (encouragement to all 'ordinary' musicians and ministers) but was brought on by Jack Buchanan, the Scottish singer, local boy from Helensburgh, where I live and this book was written. Her great successes included 'Goodnight Vienna' (1932), and 'Bittersweet' (1933) - that dated old world again! Yet one of her finest roles was her least glamorous, that of 'Odette' (1950), set in the black realism of disfigured modernity.

But here is a final serendipity. She was not, after all, speaking 'live' to me. The programme was recorded. Now biologically dead, she, like Lenny Bernstein, lives in the alchemy of tape and film. And her autobiography is entitled 'There's Always Tomorrow'.

Indeed there is. Equally, there's always yesterday. They meet today. Which is our golden opportunity!